Marxist Left Review

Number 30 – Autumn 2026

Editor
Omar Hassan

Editorial committee
Mick Armstrong
Sandra Bloodworth
Omar Hassan
Louise O'Shea

Reviews editor
Alexis Vassiley

© Social Research Institute

Published by Socialist Alternative
Melbourne, April 2026

PO Box 4354
Melbourne University, VIC 3052

www.marxistleftreview.org

marxistleftreview@gmail.com

Contributions to *Marxist Left Review* are peer-reviewed

ISSN 1838-2932
rrp. $20

Subediting and proofreading
Tess Lee Ack
Diane Fieldes

Layout and production
Susan Miller
Luka Kiernan

Cover
Susan Miller

Printed by IngramSpark

Marxist Left Review is a theoretical journal published twice-yearly by Socialist Alternative, a revolutionary organisation based in Australia.

We aim to engage with theoretical and political debates on the Australian and international left, making a rigorous yet accessible case for Marxist politics. We also seek to provide analysis of the social, political and economic dynamics shaping Australian capitalism.

Unless indicated otherwise all articles published reflect the views of the individual author(s).

We rely on our readers' support to continue publication.
You can help by subscribing at *marxistleftreview.org*

Marxist Left Review

Number 30 – Autumn 2026

TOM BRAMBLE

Editorial: Australia catches up: Understanding One Nation's far right surge

Tom Bramble has published widely on political economy and the labour movement and is a regular contributor to *Marxist Left Review*. His recent books include *Introducing Marxism: A Theory of Social Change* and *The Fight for Workers' Power: Revolution and Counter-Revolution in the 20th Century* (with Mick Armstrong).

WE ARE NOW at a watershed in Australian politics, the most dramatic developments for decades. The entire political order that has governed Australia for more than a century – the alternation in government of Labor and Liberal-National parties (and their predecessors) – is crumbling. While important developments are under way on the left of politics, with the ALP's primary vote sinking steadily, the most dramatic change has been a radicalisation of the right. Support for the Liberal Party, the preferred party of the capitalist class, has been dropping for two decades but is now collapsing.

A catalyst for this latest turn and its chief beneficiary has been One Nation, now overtaking the Coalition in the polls. With the far right pushing ahead of the established centre-right parties, Australia is now catching up with much of Europe, where centrist parties have been hammered by the far right since the 1990s. The speed at which Australia is doing so is astonishing, suggesting that processes in this direction have been under way for years but awaiting an outlet around which far-right sentiments could coalesce. One Nation has now become that outlet. Any number of developments may follow; the very future of the Liberal Party is in question.

The Bondi massacre in December was an accelerant to trends already under way: the hardening of the right and increased state repression of civil liberties.

The situation demands resistance on every front which puts a premium on building a much bigger socialist left. "Business as usual" is not an option. If the right is radicalising, we need a radicalisation on the left. Labor's sinking primary vote and paralysis in the Greens opens the space for socialists to grow, but we can only do so if we seize the opportunity.

How did we get to this moment?

The Liberals may have seen their support collapse in a few short months, but the roots of the crisis lie in the defeat of the Howard government in 2007.

John Howard, prime minister from 1996 to 2007 and the party's second longest-serving leader, created a right-wing Liberal Party, driving out many of the party's so-called "moderates". He brought together a right-wing electoral constituency that allowed him to win four straight elections, thanks in part to rising living standards underpinned by the mining boom.

Howard was able to use his authority to discipline the party and hold One Nation at bay. Following the 1998 breakthrough by One Nation in Queensland, when the party scored 23 percent of the vote and won 11 seats, threatening the Nationals in their heartlands, Howard convinced the Liberals and Nationals to put One Nation last on their how-to-vote cards. This, along with Howard's adoption of many of Hanson's policies, determined left-wing protests to prevent One Nation making inroads into Victoria, and One Nation's internal shambles, sent the party into reverse for several years. The Liberals and Nationals were able to re-cohere their right-wing base in the regional and rural areas while Howard's tax cuts kept the party's affluent metropolitan base happy.

The Howard government was eventually destroyed by overreach, as it attacked working-class living standards through its 2005 WorkChoices industrial laws. The resulting backlash cost the prime minister not just government but his own seat at the 2007 election.

Since 2007, the Liberals have been thrashing around, trying to recreate their glory days. The Coalition was returned to office in 2013 and the conservatives won the following two elections. But the Liberals' internal leadership churn – Brendan Nelson, Malcolm Turnbull, Tony Abbott, Malcolm Turnbull again, followed by Scott Morrison – told the real story. Whether "moderate" or hard right, they have failed to find a leader with mass appeal, something only reinforced by then opposition leader Peter Dutton's spectacular failure at the 2025 federal election.

The failure of party leaders to command authority has made it harder for the party to hold together its electoral base. There has always been significant support for the hard right in regional and rural areas which have been the basis of support for a string of right-wing extremist organisations going back more than a century. The most important elements of this strand of Australian politics have been antisemitism, anti-socialism, anti-trade unionism, white supremacy and support for crown and empire. For many decades the Liberal and National parties were able to hegemonise this layer. Gradually, however, they lost their grip on these people to right-wing micro-parties, some little more than vanity projects, who took advantage of disillusionment with the mainstream parties and notched up quite substantial votes at the conservatives' expense.

On top of the traditional anxieties and hatreds widespread among these regional and rural voters, the far right today feeds on their sense of abandonment, the closure of regional facilities as populations shrink, an increasingly multicultural immigration intake shaking their conception of what it means to be Australian, challenges to gender and family roles, the covid pandemic and associated emergency measures to deal with the virus. Trump's presidential victories in the US have confirmed in the minds of the far right that their cause is just and right, reinforced by right-wing, US-owned social media companies and Murdoch's Sky after Dark, which direct a curated diet of right-wing conspiracy theories into their newsfeeds.

The far right has also made inroads in the outer suburbs of the major cities in recent years. Here, it is likely that economic insecurity associated with a cost-of-living crisis and housing unaffordability has been a factor undermining support for both the major parties. While many of this layer might once have voted Labor, the party's enthusiastic embrace of neoliberalism in the 1980s and the failure of the unions to fight for working-class interests has seen them defect to the right. Labor's demonisation of refugees and its targeting of immigrants as pushing up house prices created an environment in which open racism has become normalised.

The Liberal Party has shifted steadily to the right to try to capture these voters. In doing so they are following a path trodden by many of their formerly centre-right partners overseas. In a world increasingly characterised by chaos, militarism, irrationalism and growing disenchantment with the record of centre-right governments in office, the far right have promoted themselves as an alternative by popularising authoritarian, blood and soil politics, targeting immigrants, socialists and, in today's parlance, woke policies for weakening the nation.

The centre-right parties have prepared the way for the far right with their own anti-immigration policies which, far from providing a buffer against the far right, only legitimise them. And while the centre-right parties may initially refuse to form coalitions or election pacts with the far right, little by little, the barriers to partnership have been dismantled. In the case of the United States, this process has taken place within the Republican Party but in Europe and Latin America, the process more commonly involves the rise to power of new right-wing parties.

This process of right-wing radicalisation may have been slowed in Australia to some degree by a lesser degree of social polarisation associated with four decades of unbroken economic growth. However, pressures in this direction have been building up over that time, evident in the votes garnered by far-right parties at successive federal elections.

The Liberal Party membership has also been drifting rightwards as it shrinks and ages. The party itself has shrunk dramatically over many decades and membership now stands at around 25,000, one sixth of the figure in the mid-1970s when the overall population was half the size. Failing to recruit new members, the party is rapidly ageing, with average age of members now standing at 70, nearly twice as old as the median. This shrinking, ageing membership is a support base for the hard right within the party, as is evident from members' enthusiasm for John Howard, Tony Abbott, Peter Dutton and, today, Andrew Hastie and Jacinta Nampijinpa Price.

One Nation, with the biggest brand recognition on the far right, has now seized the moment. The party is potentially on the threshold of displacing the Liberals and Nationals as the main conservative force in Australian politics. Unlike the mainstream conservatives, One Nation has not held office and therefore disappointed its supporters, and since they have not been the main opposition party, have not been under pressure to respond to every policy debate that might potentially alienate sections of its base. They are filling the space of an increasingly discredited centre-right Liberal Party which in shifting right itself has only legitimised and normalised One Nation. Pauline Hanson's party can both pose as a mouthpiece of the hard right and rail against what it calls the failed duopoly of Labor and the Liberals.

Because One Nation can pick and choose where they engage, they are united in their ideological message: anti-immigration, anti-"woke", anti-socialist and anti-welfare (except for small business, farmers and mining companies). Dutton believed the Liberals could use the 2023 Indigenous Voice to Parliament referendum to whip up racism and win votes on that basis. The main beneficiary however was the far right, which seized on the campaign to radicalise its supporters and won over Liberal voters at the 2025 federal election.

It is not just on the right that the Liberals are losing their base. At the 2013 election, the Liberals won 44 metropolitan seats; they now hold just nine. Labor has picked up the majority of the party's urban seats – 28 – most in the middle and outer suburbs. But the most devastating blow to the party has been the loss of five wealthy, blue-ribbon Liberal seats in Sydney and one each in Melbourne and Perth: Wentworth, Mackellar, Warringah, Bradfield, North Sydney, Kooyong and Curtin. These are not just any seats. For many years Liberal branches in these electorates provided the party with their leaders, their front bench, their up-and-comers, their funding and their access to business executives and other channels of influence. These were the branches that mattered. Almost all of them were lost in the 2022 election, and the follow-up defeat last May– with Tim Wilson the only Liberal to grab a seat back off the teals – suggests that these seats aren't coming back to the Liberal Party any time soon. For now, at least, the socially liberal, economically neoliberal teals have stolen this element of the Liberal base, while Labor has grabbed two dozen seats in the middle and outer rings.

The problem for the Liberals is that they are now, with a few exceptions, restricted to seats in regional and rural areas but cannot win a federal election by relying solely on these seats, given two-thirds of electorates are in the cities. Combined losses in the cities to the teals and Labor mean that the Liberals now hold just 34 seats out of 150 in the lower house, half the number they had before the 2022 election. The party is left with no seats in Tasmania after last year's election. None in the ACT. None in the NT. In NSW they lost four seats, in Queensland, five and two in Tasmania. Millions spent by the Gina Rinehart-funded propaganda vehicle Advance to promote the Liberals' cause at the 2025 election did nothing to help them.

In the Senate, the Liberals (including the LNP in Queensland) hold 25 spots and the Nationals another two out of 75, as against 39 for Labor and the Greens, the biggest deficit faced by the mainstream conservatives since the 1940s.

The situation is only getting worse as depopulation of the bush sees the Liberal and National's natural constituencies lose numbers on the floor of parliament.

The Liberal Party is faring no better in state government, holding only Queensland and Tasmania. The result – leadership instability – is the same there: eight leadership changes at state or territory level since August 2024.

The Liberals are losing ground across important demographics. They have little support among young people. But nor are they winning among millennials, those in their 30s and early 40s who might once have transitioned from Labor to the Coalition as they aged. At the 2025 election, just one in five millennials voted for the Coalition. The Menzies-era Liberal Party put great store in home ownership steering voters towards the Liberal Party. That has now gone into reverse as younger voters see no reason to identify with the party advocating multibillion dollar tax breaks for property investors. Last year, the conservative parties won only two seats where more than one-third of the electorate are renters. The Coalition is becoming increasingly dependent on older voters, born during the postwar boom decades but who are now literally dying out.

Nor is the Coalition advancing in seats with migrant groups the Liberals hope to win sympathy with. In a range of seats, the Liberals have selected non-Anglo migrant candidates and assiduously worked their respective business associations, but this has not translated into votes. Of the 50 electorates with the highest migrant populations, the Liberals hold just two. Dutton's strategy of targeting No-voting outer suburban seats traditionally held by Labor on the basis of an anti-woke, economically aspirational platform came to nothing. Indeed, the Liberals went backwards in these areas.

Then there is the Liberals' "women problem", a euphemism for the party's sexism. Sussan Ley's dumping as leader after just nine months, leaving only five women in the party room, will only have reinforced this in the minds of potential Liberal voters. This, combined with the fact Labor has made women a significant focus, means the Liberals are starting from behind, with nothing to offer half the electorate. Liberal support among university-educated women in white-collar jobs, an increasingly important element of the workforce, is minimal – of the top 20 electorates by percentage of professional women, the Liberals hold just one.

The mainstream conservatives are in crisis, then, because they are losing two key constituencies, in the cities and in regional and rural areas. The more the Liberals swing further to the right in an attempt to hold on to the latter, the more they are likely to alienate the former. But judging from the experience of the Turnbull leadership, and, today, Ley, positioning as "moderates" won't win the teal supporters back either. And, when push comes to shove, the "moderates" capitulate to the hard right of the party every time. It was the moderate Turnbull who as prime minister not only carried out traditional pro-capitalist policies like cutting corporate tax, removing restrictions on concentration of media ownership and reintroducing the anti-union

Australian Building and Construction Commission but who also blocked the introduction of marriage equality for two years. It was Ley who in her last weeks in office went full Trump, drawing up an immigration program barring citizens from countries supposedly hosting Islamist terrorist groups.

The Bondi massacre and its aftermath

Support for the Liberals has been weakening for years. One Nation has been steadily climbing in the polls for more than a year. Government repression of protest movements, in particular the climate movement but more recently Palestine demonstrations, has been increasing. But the Bondi massacre and the ruling-class offensive against the Palestine movement that followed have brought things to a boil.

Ever since the first demonstrations were called in solidarity with Palestine on 9 October 2023, the ruling class has been attacking the movement for supposedly making Jews feel "unsafe". The media have uncritically regurgitated every story of supposed antisemitic attack and sheeted home blame for them to the weekly Palestine solidarity demonstrations in Sydney and Melbourne. They have slandered the movement as "extremist" and invoked "social cohesion" to try to silence protests.

The Bondi Beach massacre gave the ruling class an opportunity to ratchet up pressure on the movement. While the offensive was initiated by the Coalition parties, One Nation, the Executive Council of Australian Jewry, the Zionist Federation and the Murdoch press, it was quickly taken up by a broad spectrum of ruling-class bodies, including big business lobby groups, former heads of security agencies and armed forces, judges and barristers, the editors of the ABC and Nine newspapers and university vice-chancellors.

The right-wing offensive cohered on a series of demands: full implementation of the Segal Report recommendations, a set of McCarthyite measures aimed in particular at the universities and ABC, a royal commission into antisemitism and legislation to criminalise so-called "hate speech" and "hate groups", by which they meant the Palestine solidarity campaign.

The ruling class has made some important gains out of its despicable weaponisation of the Bondi massacre. Having initially opposed a royal commission into antisemitism and social cohesion, the Albanese government agreed to it, with hearings already under way. The right will now use the royal commission hearings to demand a crackdown on the Palestine movement and attack immigrants. The widening of powers of the security agencies that will undoubtedly result from the royal commission will allow the police and security forces greater leeway to attack the freedoms of the Palestine campaign to organise.

The Albanese government has agreed to implement all the recommendations of the Segal report, to accept the IHRA definition of antisemitism, and to pass hate speech laws. It invited the Israeli president, Isaac Herzog to visit Australia to reinforce good relations with the apartheid state. The Minns government banned street demonstrations in Sydney and orchestrated a savage attack by 3,500 riot police against a demonstration called by the Palestine Action Group (PAG) to protest Herzog's visit.

State Labor governments in Victoria and WA are moving ahead with laws to give the police greater powers to restrict demonstrations. The Crisafulli LNP government in Queensland has introduced legislation to prohibit even the expression of pro-Palestine slogans.

It is unclear exactly how things will pan out in coming months, but the frenzied media campaign against PAG and, specifically, organiser Josh Lees, suggests that the Palestine movement will be squarely in the sights of state and federal governments. How much the university vice-chancellors will prosecute Palestine activism on campus, a particular animus of the right-wing campaign, will be clearer in coming months. We don't know how much the NSW Police and Minns government will regard the police riot in Sydney as a model for future responses; for now, the restrictions on Palestine demonstrations have been lifted. Regardless of short-term considerations, it is easy to foresee how this machinery of repression will be rolled out against any movement in future challenging Australia's involvement in a US war in Asia or against striking trade unionists.

The ruling class has not had it all its own way since the Bondi massacre. The Palestine movement refuses to be cowed by the ruling-class offensive. Few were prepared to sign on to a campaign supposedly to combat racism that featured figures like John Howard, Pauline Hanson and Tony Abbott. So, when the board of the South Australian Writers Festival, on the orders of premier Peter Malinauskas, cancelled Randa Abdel-Fattah's appearance at the Adelaide Writers' Festival in January, it was heartening but no surprise to see the majority of other invited speakers pull out, wrecking the festival.

The ruling class believed they could use Herzog's visit to rebuild Israel's image in public opinion and to marginalise the Palestine movement. But it wasn't difficult to see the cynicism involved in a tour by a man who had signed IDF missiles and declared the entire population of Gaza military targets. The Palestine movement struck back, organising rallies in 26 towns and cities to protest the visit. Tens of thousands came out on demonstrations across the country. The Minns government's violent attack on the Sydney demonstration meant that the media story of the week was not happy photo ops of Herzog meeting school children and glad-handing politicians but mass opposition on the streets to the Israeli president.

The resilience and defiance of the Palestine movement should not, however, make us overlook the dominant feature of the political landscape: the radicalisation of the right.

While Ley may have made the running in the early days after the Bondi massacre, her demand for hate speech legislation backfired on the Coalition. The Liberals, under pressure from the ruling class and Israel's supporters to pass the Albanese government's bill, supported it after doing their best to ensure it could not be used to target racists. The Nationals, keen to keep the faith with unapologetic racists and to prevent a further drift of support to One Nation, opposed it. The Coalition split for a second time and then again reunited but on an even more right-wing basis. Disastrous polling for the Liberals in the face of One Nation's rise was the catalyst for a leadership spill, resulting in Ley's replacement by the hard right's Angus Taylor, who immediately raised anti-immigration and Muslim-bashing rhetoric and appointed right-wing warriors Hastie and Price to his shadow Cabinet. Should Taylor fail to lift polling for the Liberals he in turn will be replaced by Hastie or a similar figure from the party's far right, confirming an almost complete ideological convergence with One Nation.

The Liberals' recent internal disarray and continued drift to the right is in large part a function of One Nation's success. Hanson's party now regularly runs second in polling, drawing support primarily from the mainstream right parties. If One Nation can turn polling support into votes, it could become the second largest party in federal and many state parliaments. That would be the most dramatic shift in Australian politics since the formation of the ALP in the 1890s.

Far from moderating its political stance as their support has soared, One Nation has become even more extreme, dispensing with the niceties of the soft racist distinction between "good Muslims" and "bad Muslims" to denounce the entire religion and its practitioners. Every other right-wing cause – reducing immigration, especially from Muslim and other "brown" nations, the flag, the national anthem, the armed forces, Australia Day, men's rights, anti-vaccination – is now being deployed by One Nation as it seeks to consolidate its new position as a catch-all party of the entire far right in Australia.

The Liberals and Nationals are now at risk of being wiped out by One Nation. That is the imminent threat and one the Liberals are countering by pushing further to the right to try to win back defectors to One Nation. At the forthcoming Farrer by-election, all three parties will be fielding candidates. In that sense the traditional conservative parties are in a fight for their lives. But whoever wins, the rightward shift in Australian politics will continue. More unites them than divides them: all three are racist, nationalist, militarist, anti-welfare, pro-Trump, anti-union and anti-socialist. That Barnaby Joyce, once deputy prime minister and leader of the National Party, could decamp to One Nation without any obvious change of political line demonstrates that all three parties are cut from the same cloth. More defections are likely, as we are witnessing senior Tories jumping over to Nigel Farage's Reform UK. A realignment of the right-wing parties, the better to take the fight to the Albanese government, is by no means ruled out.

How can we fight the right?

Over the course of One Nation's life, the dominant liberal response has been to denounce Hanson as a simple-minded bigot and to argue against any mobilisations against her on the basis that they would just "draw attention to her" or "give her oxygen". Others comforted themselves, with somewhat more justification, that she should just be ignored because her movement would collapse, as it has done several times since its formation in 1997.

These arguments were an excuse for passivity. There was no basis to suggest that by not protesting she would be denied publicity; the entire spectrum of media gave her intensive coverage in the late 1990s, transforming her from a minor independent on the floor of parliament to a national figure. Several factors were responsible, but it cannot be denied that big protests outside planned Hanson public meetings in Victoria played a role in cruelling her attempt to break through in that state in the late 1990s.

Today, the argument to "just ignore" One Nation is more dangerous. One Nation is no longer a noisy but minor force in national politics. It is pulling support in the mid-20s across the country. The party is attracting funding from the country's richest person, Gina Rinehart, and a growing cohort of other capitalists. With its reach and funding, One Nation is in a better position to set up stable structures with competent organisers. This is not to say it will sustain its current level of support; it could stabilise or fall back. But even if One Nation did collapse, that would not be the end of the far right. The Liberals and Nationals are both going in that direction anyway, in line with their peers across the world.

Any idea we can look to the Liberals and Nationals as a bulwark against One Nation is evidently a dead end and should not need saying. But unfortunately, it does. Some figures in and around the ALP have argued recently that progressives must "throw our votes behind the Liberal", as former NSW premier Bob Carr put it in relation to the Farrer by-election where Labor has no chance of winning. This will supposedly send a message to migrants and international observers that "race prejudice" is unwelcome in Australia. But this approach is a dead end. How does voting for a Liberal candidate anywhere help beat back racism when the entire party is chock full of racists and elected representatives are bound by the party caucus to vote for the racist bill of fare that now forms the Liberal program? While socialists advocate putting One Nation last, this in no sense involves relying on the Liberals or Nationals to fight Hanson & Co. We need to fight all the parties of the right. And that means building a bigger left alternative.

Nor can Labor be a defence against the rise of the far right. Support for Labor has held up in the polls since the last election but this is not out of any love for the party or its leaders, it is rather a function of widespread antipathy towards the opposition. Despite its electoral dominance the ALP is possibly the weakest it has ever been, undermined by its much-diminished membership and a decrepit union movement that seems incapable of doing anything other than posting on social media, all made worse by its decades of right-wing policies. This has resulted in extremely low party loyalty, as seen in its historically low primary vote.

Whether in opposition or in office, Labor pursues an uninspiring program that is incapable of responding to the widespread disgust towards the status quo. Labor's nationalism, its racist immigration policies and Islamophobia, its anti-protest laws and its military expansionism and slavish loyalty to the US only reinforce and legitimise right-wing positions. The Albanese government's callous response to the plight of the so-called "ISIS brides" and their children, stuck in horrific conditions in Syrian camps, demonstrates that Labor's reaction to the rise of One Nation is to ape them, not fight them.

Nor do the Greens offer any real solution to the rise of Hanson and the right. For the past two or three years, their modus operandi has been to do deals with Labor and to promote themselves as a party of progressive liberalism, part of respectable society. This tendency only accelerated after Adam Bandt and Queensland MHR Max Chandler-Mather lost their seats at last year's election, leaving in charge Larissa Waters, the epitome of milquetoast liberalism. The Greens' desire not to rock the boat was demonstrated by their decision to back the antisemitism royal commission.

Chandler-Mather and close ally Jonathan Sriranganathan have both criticised the Greens' recent trajectory and argued for a more fighting stance. But while this might appeal to young white-collar workers being squeezed by rising rents who might once have voted Labor, it runs up against the interests of a significant element of the party's constituency of middle-aged home-owning professionals with whom the Greens compete for votes with the teals. Trying to straddle these two constituencies prevents the Greens from giving a clear anti-capitalist lead, one that might involve strikes and picket lines that would give courage to our side and demoralise the right. The Greens have simply failed to capitalise on the political turmoil of the past 12 months, their polling remaining static. The contrast with the Greens in the UK, who have built out of disillusionment with the Starmer Labour government, is obvious.

To push back the right, we need to fight them, and this fight needs to have at its centre working-class politics and action. The current trade union leaders, loyal as they are to the Labor Party, will not lead this fight. They refuse to mobilise against One Nation, excusing themselves with the argument that many of their members support the party and will quit the union if it attacks them. Better stick to the bread-and-butter demands for higher wages and better conditions that all workers can support, they argue. But union leaders are not even doing that. They are failing on both fronts. They have quashed strikes and collective struggle for years, and refuse to oppose seriously Labor policy, even when it means remaining silent about a genocide. They have sat on their hands as the cost-of-living crisis rolls on into its fifth year, and their refusal to organise strikes has allowed the bosses to get away with murder.

This leaves the considerable number of people who want higher wages and are willing to do something to get them, who are disgusted by genocide backed by Western powers, and who want to see money going to health and education rather than nuclear submarines, without any mainstream leadership. This is the constituency the Socialist Party is attempting to connect with and give hope to. It is both a strength and a weakness that this left pole is currently largely unorganised and without credible leadership: it is less influenced by the apologists for the system that dominate official politics, but also it is a huge endeavour to begin to organise this layer into a political force that can make an impact on the political landscape. This is why involving more people in socialist organising is such an urgent priority: we need an anti-capitalist force that argues for working-class unity against racism, for improving living standards through unity in action against the bosses and their servants in Canberra, and that shows the real power workers have, which means we do not have to rely on political "leaders" in parliament or the unions to change things for us—we have that power ourselves.

This, then, tells us the priorities for our side. There is no point bemoaning the failure of the centre to hold back the far right. The sustained anti-war movement that has mobilised on our streets for well over two years and the widespread disgust at the Albanese government rolling out the welcome mat to Herzog tell us that millions are pissed off with what's currently on offer. The continued turn-up at Invasion Day rallies despite the loss of the Albanese government's insipid Voice to Parliament referendum shows that people will resist racism even if the government won't. Across the country, the Socialist Party is preparing to mobilise for local, state and federal elections in the coming years to put up a real challenge to the ALP and Greens. If you want to be part of resisting the rise of the right and fighting for a working-class alternative, there has never been a better time to get involved.

MICK ARMSTRONG

Why Pauline Hanson's rise is different from last time

Mick Armstrong is the co-author of *The Labor Party: a Marxist Analysis* and *The Fight for Workers' Power: Revolution and Counter-Revolution in the 20th Century*, and has written widely on revolutionary organisation and the Australian labour movement.

ANYONE WHO BELIEVED that "easy going" Australia was somehow immune from the far-right tide that has swept across Europe and the US has been confounded by the rapid surge in support for One Nation, which has now overtaken the combined vote of the Liberals and Nationals in various opinion polls.

Over the last two decades the tendency on the left has been to dismiss Pauline Hanson as a "has been" and a joke. We can no longer afford that attitude. The rules of the game have decisively changed. We are in a much more volatile and threatening international political situation, with Trump in the White House and long entrenched bulwarks of the Western political establishment such as the British Tory party threatened with annihilation as much of its voter base defects to Nigel Farage's far-right Reform UK. There are no grounds for complacency. Politics has become much more serious and the left needs to rise to the occasion and offer a clear alternative to defend working-class interests.

Hanson first rose to prominence back in 1996, with an inflammatory maiden speech to parliament condemning Aboriginal people and proclaiming that "White Australia" was being swamped by

Asian immigration.[1] For months the petty-bourgeois fish and chip shop owner was the darling of the media, which dwelt on her every word and published her racist diatribe in full. Any protest against Hanson was condemned as an attack on "free speech". The Liberals and the Nationals lapped it all up and Labor leader Kim Beasley refused to call Hanson a racist.

Hanson, like so many far-right and fascist figures in Australian history, had emerged out of the bowels of the Liberal Party. She was the pre-selected Liberal candidate for the Ipswich-based seat of Oxley for the 1996 elections. However her vile attacks on Aboriginal people were too embarrassing even for hard-nosed Liberal operatives. She was disendorsed at the last minute but with the help of local Liberal Party members went on to win as an independent. Hanson benefited from the economic hardship that had hit the rural middle class. With un-employment at nearly 9 percent there was widespread disillusionment with the Keating Labor government, which had turned its back on its working-class supporters.

The newly elected prime minister, John Howard, was determined to shift society sharply to the right. Howard saw Hanson as a useful ally in his campaign against "political correctness" – right-wing code for any opposition to racism or bigotry. Howard implemented many of Hanson's policies – cutting immigration, especially family reunions, locking up refugees, extinguishing Native Title, abolishing the Aboriginal and Torres Strait Islander Commission (ATSIC) and disbanding the Office of Multicultural Affairs.

It was only when One Nation began to severely erode the Liberal Party vote and cost it seats that Howard's sympathy for Hanson began to fade. The 1998 Queensland state election was an important turning point. The Liberals directed preferences to One Nation but it backfired badly on them. One Nation won 22 percent of the vote and captured a swag of Liberal seats, and by splitting the conservative vote delivered a range of other seats to Labor.

Rising mass opposition to Hanson also worried Howard and sections of the ruling class. Initially most workers in the major urban

---

1   For an overview of the fight against Hanson last time round see Lee Ack 2016.

centres were shocked and intimidated by the media barrage championing Hanson. But fear quickly turned to anger and loathing as a clearer understanding of the nature of Hanson's right-wing agenda seeped in. With her backing from top mining bosses like Hugh Morgan and the Murdoch press, class-conscious workers saw her as a serious threat to their rights. In response to rank-and-file pressure trade union officials in Melbourne organised a 50,000-strong anti-racism rally.

In that context the confrontational protests that targeted and on a number of occasions actually shut down One Nation meetings had a real impact. They helped to cohere anti-racists and gave them confidence that they were not alone. They demonstrated to the migrant communities that were under attack that there was a reservoir of opposition to Hanson's racism, and that something could be done to push back against it. The protests also played a key role in breaking the momentum of her movement, demoralising her supporters and preventing Hanson establishing strongholds outside rural areas.[2] Significantly, support for One Nation was weakest in Victoria, where the protests against Hanson were most intense, collapsing to just 2 percent in mid-1998.

For over two years Australia was gripped by one of the most sustained and militant protest movements since the end of the Vietnam War. However the role of the mass protests in breaking the back of the Hanson upsurge in the 1990s has been almost totally written out of history. Our rulers and their supporters in the media and the ALP don't want you to realise that by standing up and fighting back you can begin to change the world. They want you to calm down and "lower the temperature", as Anthony Albanese constantly declares; leave it to those in authority, parliamentarians, judges, police and their ilk to supposedly resolve the situation.

In Hawthorn, with just five days notice, Socialist Alternative initiated a 3,000-strong mobilisation that shut down Hanson's meeting. In working-class suburbs like Melbourne's Dandenong anti-Hanson protests mobilised not just the far left but many thousands of local Asian and white workers. These militant protests helped spark a

---

2   Sparrow 1997.

much broader anti-racist movement, with large walkouts of school students that spread to numerous regional centres and country towns. Hundreds of Aboriginal people clashed with police in Echuca during an anti-Hanson protest. Rockhampton had a sizeable demonstration and 5,000 rallied in Bendigo.

The confrontational protests were, of course, denounced in the press and by all the "respectable" forces in society, including ALP leaders. Mealy-mouthed small-l liberal types also criticised the protests. They claimed the protests were just giving Hanson more publicity and driving people into her arms. But the evidence pointed to the opposite conclusion: whenever Hanson was confronted with disruptive protests, support for her fell in the opinion polls. Those outside her hard-core base drifted away from her.

Small-l liberals looked down on Hanson as ignorant and uneducated. She had not been to the right private school and been taught a more sophisticated form of pro-capitalist politics. They feared her crude racism would embarrass Australia on the international stage. They did not attack her important role as an agent of the bosses attempting to shore up support for the capitalist system by deflecting discontent onto migrants, Aboriginal people and other scapegoats. The small-l liberals' sneering elitism offered no strategy for defeating the far right. Indeed they were just as sneering about socialists who played a prominent role in leading the fightback against One Nation as they were about Hanson.

The mass anti-Hanson mobilisations broke the back of a genuinely threatening far-right movement and prevented the consolidation of a serious fascist organisation. The 1980s had seen substantial far-right street mobilisations, such as the "Save Australia" rally backed by the Herald Sun against the Victorian "socialist Fabian government". Support for the reactionary "Joh [Bjelke Petersen] for Canberra" campaign peaked at 27 percent in 1987. By 1996 far-right support was surging, with over 70,000 marching in Melbourne to oppose Howard's gun laws.

An array of fascist organisations, including National Action and its skinhead gangs, coalesced around Hanson, who they saw as their "great white hope". Hanson herself was becoming more extreme, publishing a book, *The Truth*, accusing Aboriginal people of cannibalism. But in the face of the mass mobilisations and the waning of ruling-class support, One Nation was wracked with infighting and corruption scandals and tore itself apart. The eleven One Nation MPs elected in Queensland in 1998 deserted the party.

In the 1990s the mainstream media, innumerable liberal commentators and some on the left repeatedly claimed that Hanson's support base was overwhelmingly working-class "racist rednecks". Some conservative workers, especially in rural areas, did vote One Nation. However Hanson overwhelmingly attracted former Coalition voters, not Labor voters. Opinion polls in the 1990s showed that it was unionised workers who were most hostile to Hanson.

Like many far-right movements, her core supporters were drawn from the small town middle class of real estate agents, pharmacists, lawyers, accountants, dentists and bank managers.[3] They in turn galvanised around them retirees, police, sections of the self-employed, long-term unemployed and non-unionised workers in small workplaces. One Nation's highest votes were in small town rural areas, peaking at 43.5 percent in Bjelke Petersen's old electorate of Barambah in south-east Queensland.

In the capital cities, as the commentator Phillip Adams noted, BMW and Volvo owners were prominent at Hanson's meetings, not struggling blue-collar workers.[4] As Australia is one of the most urbanised and proletarianised societies in the world, One Nation's failure in the 1990s to make significant inroads into the urban working class marginalised her movement. Whether One Nation or another far-right force can seriously consolidate a presence in the capital cities this time round will be decisive.

Right up to the present day, One Nation's leaders and candidates have overwhelmingly had a background as managers, small business owners or at times quite substantial capitalists. David Farley, One Nation's Farrer by-election candidate, is a former CEO of the

---

3   Lee Ack 2016, p.23.

4   See Armstrong 1998 for a detailed analysis of the One Nation vote in the 1998 Queensland state election, their most successful election campaign.

Australian Agricultural Company, one of Australia's largest cattle producers. One Nation Senator Malcolm Roberts was the general manager of the Gordonstone coal mine. Western Australian One Nation Senator Tyron Whitten owns a construction business. Hanson herself is estimated to have a $20 million fortune.

One Nation has if anything moved further to the right since the 1990s, doubling down on its anti-Asian racism. A typical example was One Nation's Victorian state secretary Bianca Colecchia posting a video of people in Melbourne's CBD on New Year's Eve, exclaiming: "Spot the Westerner?" Vilifying Muslims is stock-in-trade for Hanson. She has embraced every fascist-style cause: championing Donald Trump, denouncing life-saving vaccines and the World Health Organization, opposing abortion rights, backing "men's rights" and nuclear power combined with climate denialism. One Nation's website calls for an end to "net zero" because "it is a vehicle for creating a socialist Australia in which citizens are forced under comprehensive government control".

Despite all this, there is nothing like the popular hostility to Hanson that was so widespread in the 1990s. She has to a considerable extent been normalised by the media and the political establishment while gaining the support of some of the wealthiest Australian capitalists, including Gina Reinhart. Official politics have moved further and further to the right. The Liberal Party preferenced One Nation in the South Australian elections, while Labor Prime Minister Anthony Albanese recently officially met up with Hanson for the first time.

Part of the reason that Hanson does not seem so extreme is that both Labor and the Liberals have implemented some of her most reactionary policies on refugees and asylum seekers and hostility to workers' rights. Both mainstream parties have repeatedly whipped up Islamophobia, implemented a law-and-order agenda that targeted Aboriginal people and African migrants and backed the genocide in Gaza, while undermining basic health services and workers' living standards to boost the profits of big business. In this context anti-immigration sentiment has grown, while support for action to confront climate change has fallen significantly.

International trends have also had an important impact, with the far right becoming an established force in country after country. Sections of the capitalist class have been enthused by the success of Trump and Farage. Rupert Murdoch's Sky News and the Australian have played a key role in consolidating far-right talking points on a range of issues like climate change and support for Israel. They have helped develop a cadre of far-right and openly fascist influencers. They have fuelled support for the likes of Jacinta Price and Andrew Hastie on the extreme right of the Liberal Party as well as for Hanson.

In many rural areas and regional centres, especially in NSW and Queensland, support for far-right politics has been consolidated over a number of years. One Nation is now making inroads into urban areas. As well as taking votes from the Nationals and Liberals and to a lesser extent Labor, One Nation, which obtained 5.7 percent at the last Senate election, is soaking up the votes of the far-right microparties which between them polled 6.9 percent. A further worrying sign is that One Nation has gained a massive surge of followers on social media over the last six months. It will take a major political mobilisation to push back this threat.

Along with Barnaby Joyce, One Nation's prominence has attracted a cohort of sordid bigots and reactionary wannabes from various far-right microparties and the circles around Sky News. Adam Giles, the former Country Liberal Party Northern Territory chief minister who presided over the abuse of Aboriginal children in the Don Dale detention centre, is typical of this crew. After losing office Giles became a Sky News host, notoriously running a favourable interview with Blair Cottrell, the head of the openly Nazi United Patriots Front. Today – surprise, surprise – Giles is employed by Gina Rinehart as chief executive officer of Hancock Agriculture and S. Kidman & Co.

Heading the One Nation upper house ticket for the South Australian elections is Cory Bernardi. A former Liberal senator, Bernardi has argued for tougher anti-worker industrial relations laws, denied global warming and declared that permitting same-sex marriage would lead to legalised polygamy and bestiality. After abandoning the Liberals Bernardi, an associate of the fascist Q Society and a supporter of Dutch far-right leader Geert Wilders, formed the

Australian Conservatives. When that venture flopped he naturally became a Sky News commentator.

Another recycled bigot rallying to One Nation is former Liberal MP Bernie Finn. He was expelled from the Liberals for "a series of inflammatory social media posts" including calling for abortion to be made illegal in all circumstances and comparing Labor premier Dan Andrews to Adolf Hitler. A Trump backer who rails against the "rampant socialism" that has taken over Victoria, Finn has been a member of pretty much every conceivable far-right party, from Family First to the DLP.

There is great turmoil and reorganisation taking place in right-wing politics. The surge in support for One Nation has sharpened the crisis in the conservative parties, which shows no sign of being resolved any time soon. Exactly how things will develop over the coming months is far from clear. Despite One Nation regularly polling over 20 percent of the vote Hanson has not as yet demonstrated the capacity to build and maintain a far-right movement on anything like the scale of Farage in Britain or Le Pen in France. In the 1990s Hanson failed to develop a network of strong branches. Her new party, despite its initial electoral successes, was plagued by splits and defections. This time round One Nation is attempting to build a solid branch structure. How successful it will be it is too early to tell.

One Nation is ramping up its attempt to break through in Victoria where it has long been weakest. It has been on a recruitment drive and is establishing local branches and plans to run in every seat in the Victorian state elections this November. Given the deep unpopularity of the Allan Labor government, there is a serious danger that One Nation could obtain the balance of power in the upper house. Of course favourable opinion polls don't guarantee strong votes for Hanson on election day. Nevertheless the threat she poses should not be discounted.

One Nation is far from being the only threat. The Liberal and National parties have also shifted well to the right, partly inspired by Trump and Farage and in response to the pressure from One Nation. New Liberal leader Angus Taylor seems set to move the party further to the right, while Andrew Hastie waits in the wings itching for full Trumpification.

At the end of last year we also saw a brief flurry of racist street protests in which the openly Nazi National Socialist Network played a leading role. However the far-right sentiment at this stage is primarily electorally focused and has not led to anything like the scale of violent attacks on migrants that have repeatedly occurred in Europe. The far-right terrorist attack on the Perth Invasion Day rally is, however, a dangerous warning sign. And in the wake of Bondi there has been an increasing number of attacks on Muslims, especially Muslim women.

The far right internationally have entrenched themselves as a serious political force – dominating the US Republican party, in government in Italy, India, Israel and Hungary and leading the polls in Britain and France. Reactionary Nazi-style attitudes are widespread among sections of the US capitalist class and key operatives in the Trump administration. Elon Musk is in no sense alone in openly championing fascists. Australia is now rapidly going down the same road.

The far right is not simply some bizarre anomaly separate from capitalism. It is an integral part of the capitalist system. Fascism is a force the capitalist class has repeatedly turned to when it has suited their needs – not necessarily to take power as in Mussolini's Italy or Hitler's Germany, but as an auxiliary force to back up bourgeois power and push politics in a harsher, more authoritarian direction. This is vital to understand. Fighting fascism can't be separated from the broader fight against capitalism and the mainstream political parties whose racist and reactionary policies give the far right succour.

Fighting the far right doesn't just mean combatting them on the streets. The left must also prioritise standing up for workers' rights, opposing imperialist war, mobilising in support of Palestine, defending democratic rights, building strong socialist election campaigns. Indeed every fight in which our side stands up against the rich and powerful is essential to combatting and offering an alternative to the far right.

As long as capitalism exists there will continue to be a space for the far right to grow. As the capitalist system moves deeper into social and political crisis that space is set to expand. We can't rely on small-l liberals or reformists to consistently oppose fascism. At best the liberals will equivocate. At worst, as they have repeatedly done in the past, they will go over to the fascists, when they feel their class interests are threatened. We are in for a long fight and it is vital to build up the forces of the revolutionary left so that we can play a decisive role in the battles to come.

References

Armstrong, Mick 1998, "Who really voted for One Nation?", *Socialist Alternative* 28, July, pp.3–4.

Armstrong, Mick 2025, "The far right continues to make gains in Australia", *Red Flag*, 10 June. https://redflag.org.au/article/the-far-right-continues-to-make-gains-in-australia/

Lee Ack, Tess 2016, "How we stopped Pauline Hanson last time", *Marxist Left Review*, 12, Winter. https://marxistleftreview.org/articles/how-we-stopped-pauline-hanson-last-time/

Sparrow, Jeff 1997, "Hanson protests work!", *Socialist Alternative* 19, August, pp.3–5.

JORDAN HUMPHREYS

How capitalism – not migrants – caused Australia's housing crisis

Jordan Humphreys is an editor of *Marxist Left Review* and has written extensively on Indigenous oppression and working-class history. His book *Indigenous Liberation and Socialism* is available from Red Flag Books.

"OUR INFRASTRUCTURE IS under pressure, essential services from schools and hospitals are stretched thin. Australians are locked out of the housing market. Many are house poor, spending most of their income on rent or mortgages", explained Liberal senator Andrew Hastie in an incendiary Instagram post. "This is a housing demand crisis driven by unsustainable immigration. It's that simple. We must act."

The feeling that migrants are the cause of the housing crisis is widespread. Right-wing politicians like Hastie frequently blame "unsustainable immigration" for the lack of affordable housing. In August 2025 tens of thousands took part in the nationwide "March for Australia" rallies which called for an end to "mass migration" as a solution to the housing crisis. Pauline Hanson's racist One Nation party has been surging in the polls by making this issue its key talking point. This anti-migrant sentiment goes well beyond open racists and wannabe Trumpists. The Labor government has been pushing for caps on international students, with Treasurer Jim Chalmers claiming that "Enrolments have grown ... this puts pressure on prices and rents ... it makes finding a house harder for everyone".

Instead of challenging the racism of the Liberals and One Nation, the Albanese government has capitulated to it. Hence Albanese urged the Labor caucus to accept the idea that the March for Australia rallies were filled with "good people", unfortunately led astray by the neo-Nazis. They hoped that this would starve the issue of political oxygen. Instead, it has merely mainstreamed anti-migrant sentiment.

With most of the major political parties and the mainstream media heaping the blame for the housing crisis on migrants, it is disappointing, but not surprising, that poll after poll shows the majority of Australians want serious cuts to migration.

The real roots of the housing crisis

Blaming migration levels diverts attention from the real reasons that we are in a housing crisis. Housing in Australia is premised on the idea that houses are merely a commodity. They are something that is bought and sold, or rented, on the capitalist market. Whether you can buy a house outright, borrow to buy one over time, or rent is determined by your income. A minimal number of crumbling Housing Commission places exist only for the poorest of the poor.

Housing in Australia is deeply structured by the hierarchy of class. Data provided by the Australian Tax Office in 2023 revealed that 1 percent of taxpayers own nearly 25 percent of all investment properties in the country. While the media likes to focus on so-called "mum and dad investors", in reality only 15 percent of taxpayers in Australia are property investors. Only 21 percent of households in Australia own a property that isn't their home. Seventy-one percent of those who own more than one property only have one more. So it is a minority who own a property which isn't their own house, and then a minority of a minority that owns more than one extra property. The estimated data shows that around 50 percent of all rented housing is owned by this minority.[1]

Thirty-one percent of the population rent. A further 35 percent have their own home under a mortgage, with only 31 percent owning their home outright. The vast majority of the population don't own

---

1   Rachwani and Issa 2023.

any investment properties, and either rent or take on debt to "own" their home.[2]

Access to affordable housing is always a tense issue under capitalism. Even in the best of times, there are sections of the working class that struggle to have a secure and affordable roof over their heads. Periodically, the costs associated with housing grow dramatically, resulting in a "housing crisis". There can be a variety of reasons for this. Incomes can sharply fall or stagnate, making it harder to buy, borrow or rent. The prices of houses or rents can rise dramatically due to changes in the housing market. What all of these factors come down to is that houses are a commodity in our capitalist society. They are built in order to make money for someone. They are not a utility whose access is organised in a rational, planned and equitable way. The fluctuations in people's access to housing are but an expression of the chaotic turmoil and hierarchical structures of the capitalist markets themselves.

From the postwar housing boom to the housing crisis

Left-wing commentators often argue that the origins of our current housing crisis go back to the neoliberal turn and the subsequent decoupling of income from house prices that started in the 1980s. This was an important turning point. However, if we are to grasp why this shift took place, we have to take a longer view of the housing question in Australia.

Despite the fact that Australia is a very large country with a comparatively very small population, the lack of affordable housing has been a consistent problem, and the current housing crisis is hardly Australia's first.

Until the end of the Second World War, the federal and state governments took very little responsibility for housing. They argued that it would be wrong for the state to interfere in a private industry. Both conservative and Labor governments thought that the main thing was to entice more capitalists to invest in the risky business of constructing houses. The result was the sprawling urban slums,

---

2   ABS 2022.

decrepit amenities and crumbling housing stock that was epitomised most dramatically in Sydney.

By the 1940s, this had reached a crisis point. The shocks of the economic depressions of the 1890s and 1930s meant that capitalists were very reluctant to invest in construction. Consequently, housing stock rapidly deteriorated through the first decades of the twentieth century. By the end of the Second World War, it was estimated that Australia would need an extra 300,000–400,000 homes to house the population of a country with only 1.6 million dwellings. In NSW, it was estimated that a quarter of the population didn't have access to an adequate home in 1946.[3]

The usual story is that at this point, the heroic Labor government of Ben Chifley stepped in with a bold experimental plan to solve the housing crisis through state intervention.

The "radicalism" of the postwar Labor government's reconstruction plan has generally been exaggerated. "[F]ar from over-regulating the private sector the ALP was less interventionist than either the contemporary Labour government in Britain or the subsequent Menzies ministries in Australia", concluded economists Bob Catley and Bruce McFarlane, who pointed out that "no capital gains tax was introduced and that the percentage of GNP 'controlled by the state' only rose from 13 percent in 1941 to 14.9 percent in 1949", with a tax system significantly less progressive than Britain or Scandinavia.[4]

On the issue of housing, the postwar Labor government was even more moderate than in other policy areas. When Chifley tried to attain extra government powers via referendum in 1944, federal government control over housing was explicitly not included as an option. The Chifley government, and Chifley himself in particular, was terrified that too bold an intervention into the housing market would unite middle-class and working-class home owners against the Labor Party.

They were, however, under considerable pressure to do something about housing. The housing shortage was becoming a social crisis as the military was demobilised and marriage and birth rates spiked. A

---

3   Pullan 2019, p.22.

4   Quoted in Sheridan 1989, pp.36–7.

wave of protests, often led by returned servicemen, saw families squatting in empty or half-built homes. Underpinning this was a huge upsurge in strikes as workers pushed to end the austerity of the war years, which Labor was determined to keep going as long as possible.

The solution the Labor government hit upon, in collaboration with liberal-minded state planners and economists, was a combination of expanding public housing while leaving the rest of the housing market as unregulated as possible.

The idea was that public housing stock would be built by private construction companies who would be enticed by funding transferred from the federal government to the state governments' newly founded Housing Commissions. Workers would benefit from more stable housing, however as economists Ken Buckley and Ted Wheelwright point out, "private building contractors also gained".[5] As well, access to public housing would be restricted to those on very low incomes, so it would be put aside only for the very poorest of the poor. If not enough of the poor could be found, then the Housing Commissions were encouraged to sell off "excess" housing stock. Under Liberal Prime Minister Menzies, there was more emphasis placed on the virtues of home ownership (although he actually built more public housing faster than Chifley), and he made it easier for public housing to be sold.[6] However, the basic structure of housing was established by the postwar Labor government.

It was precisely the inadequate nature of this public housing in Australia, which was considerably worse than in Britain and western Europe, that underpinned the high rates of home ownership. In the UK almost a third of the population (29 percent) lived in public housing by the 1960s, in Germany 19.4 percent, in France around 17 percent. In Australia in 1961 it was a measly 4.2 percent. The only advanced economy that was lower at the time was the USA at 2–3 percent.[7] The

---

5   Buckley and Wheelwright 1998, p.170.

6   Troy 2011, p.3.

7   For Australia see ABS 1994 (public housing in Australia was actually at its highest in the 1990s, although still well below comparable economies). For UK and European public housing levels see Department for Communities and Local Government (UK) 2017, Scanlon and Whitehead 2011.

reality is that public housing in the UK and Western Europe today (even after decades of neoliberal restructuring and sell-offs) is still better than public housing ever was in Australia.

Most workers in Australia then simply had no other choice than to enter into the private housing market. Pullan argues that "the desire for ownership was not driven by a general suburban 'ideal' but was the population's response to an under-supplied, therefore expensive and volatile, rental market, during a time of secure, well-paid employment".[8] Under these pressures, home ownership went from 53 percent in 1947 (comparable to other advanced capitalist countries) to 70 percent by 1961 (one of the highest in the world).[9]

The expansion of both public housing and home ownership took much longer to roll out than is commonly thought. The private construction bosses dragged their feet, despite the large amounts of cash being shoved into their pockets. "The declared housing targets were never approached", writes labour historian Tom Sheridan, "and controls over prices and materials were relaxed in a manner which worked against the interests of both lower-income earners and public sector institutions".[10] A 1950 report found that housing construction in NSW was still 52 percent behind government targets and that the backlog of those requesting public housing had increased by 14 percent.[11] As time went on, the proportion of houses built that were public housing also declined.

> It had been hoped that government-sponsored housing would account for about half of all houses built, but the proportion was much smaller. In 1945–46, 4,028 houses were built under the Commonwealth-State Housing Agreement, 26 percent of the total, but by 1949–50 the proportion had fallen to 13 percent.[12]

---

8   Pullan 2019, p.84.

9   Macintyre 2020, p.227.

10   Sheridan 1989, p.176.

11   The Daily Mirror, 11 May 1950, p.16.

12   Powell and Macintyre 2015, p.162.

Throughout the 1950s and 1960s, the Australian press was still filled with articles and reports about the housing crisis in Sydney and Melbourne. There was a considerable section of the population living in "temporary dwellings", particularly in the outer suburbs of Sydney. Blocks of land were purchased with no actual house, and workers lived in makeshift dwellings on the land while they built their future home over a number of years. The 1961 census found that 45,000 people still lived in "huts and sheds".[13] There were thousands of families living in such dwellings in the early sixties. Much of our somewhat romanticised image of the postwar housing situation is really based on life during the mid-sixties to the late 1970s.

There were sections of the socialist left and the unions that were critical of the limited nature of the postwar housing plans. At the left-dominated 1945 congress of the Australian Council of Trade Unions (ACTU), criticism was raised over the government's housing policies. The Building Workers' Industrial Union (BWIU) put forward a very detailed motion calling for union representatives on the Housing Commission boards and attacking the construction bosses. In 1947, the slowness of building public housing by private construction bosses led the BWIU to demand the socialisation of the building industry. They argued that the construction and then sale of all housing should be placed under government control with union supervision. This criticism though was muted by the union leaders' sympathy for the federal Labor government and ultimate acceptance of the limits of its postwar economic plans. By 1949, all talk about socialising the building industry had evaporated, and left-wing criticism narrowed to defending the gains of the postwar Labor government against cuts by Menzies.[14]

The key issue here is that housing remained a private capitalist commodity in the postwar years. As long as incomes were rising and workers were able to afford to become homeowners, the tensions over housing, while never entirely going away, could be managed.

---

13   Pullan 2019, p.79.
14   Sheridan 1989, pp.61–2.

The turn towards neoliberalism progressively eroded the ability of the system to paper over these tensions. Government policies increasingly encouraged property investment (negative gearing, capital gains tax discounts), income inequality and indebtedness increased, and public housing and social services declined. The lack of any public control over the housing market meant that home ownership was transformed into a serious source of growing inequality, enriching some at the expense of many, renters and mortgagees alike. The end result was the decoupling of housing costs from income that is so widely discussed.

The results have been clear. In 1994–5, the proportion of households that owned their home outright was 41.8 percent; by 2025, this had dropped to 31 percent. Meanwhile, the proportion of households who were paying off a mortgage climbed from 29.6 percent to 35 percent, and renters went from 18.4 percent to 30.6 percent of households. Meanwhile, the number of households in public housing contracted from 5.5 percent to 2.9 percent.[15]

In other words, there has been a substantial decline in the number of people who own their home outright, with a significant increase in the numbers of people who are trapped in a mortgage or unable to get into home ownership. And this is just for the population overall, without breaking it down into age categories. As the Australian Institute of Health and Wellbeing (AIHW) explains, Australian home ownership rates are misleadingly inflated by the ageing population and the shift towards higher numbers of indebted home "owners". Once this is taken into account, the future trajectory of home ownership is clear.

> Home ownership among 30–34-year-olds fell from 64% in 1971 to 50% in 2021, and for 25–29-year-olds it dropped from 50% to 36%. Among those nearing retirement, home ownership also declined; for 50–54-year-olds, the rate decreased from 80% in 1996 to 72% in 2021.[16]

---

15   AIHW 2025 and ABS 2021.

16   AIHW 2025.

What is the actual impact of migration then?

Anti-immigrant crusaders can point to simple numerical facts that appear to support their arguments. After all, if there were fewer migrants there would be more houses for people to buy and rent. The problem with this argument is that it totally ignores the real relationships between wealth, ownership, inequality and housing.

To start with, it is based on the lie that housing prices, rents and interest rates are rising because migration is outstripping housing construction. However, over the last ten years, the population of Australia increased by 16 percent, while the number of houses and apartments increased by 19 percent.[17]

In 2024, Melbourne had the largest increase in net overseas migration (121,240 people), with Sydney coming in second at 120,886. Melbourne also had the largest natural increase in population as well. Despite this, housing prices in Melbourne peaked in 2021 and rose by half as much as Sydney during 2024. Brisbane (16.9 percent), Adelaide (16 percent) and Perth (23.8 percent) had the largest increases in house prices in 2024. Yet in all these states net overseas migration declined substantially that year, and of course was significantly lower than migration to Melbourne or Sydney in both raw numbers and as a percentage of the population.[18]

Drilling down into small geographical units reveals even greater variance. In NSW, a series of regional towns have had very large increases in housing prices despite stagnant population numbers or even a steady decline. Broken Hill's population declined by 0.46 percent in 2024, but housing prices in the city increased by a staggering 30 percent, the highest increase in the state. Clearly, there are other factors at work.[19]

The connection between migration and interest rate rises is even more ludicrous. The decision by the Reserve Bank to raise interest rates in February, and warn that more rises are likely, despite

---

17   Grudnoff 2025.

18   ABS 2025 and Kuru 2024.

19   Forward 2026.

migration to Australia dropping by 40 percent in the last 12 months and expected to fall further, should be proof enough.

The impact of migration on housing also can't be disentangled from the impact of migration on the economy and living standards, more generally. One of the reasons why immigration levels have been relatively high in Australia is that there has been a consistent shortage of labour, both among skilled workers and middle-class professionals, which migration has filled. This, of course, has been carried out in a thoroughly pro-capitalist manner, rather than on the basis of human rights or the free movement of people. Clearly, though, migrants have contributed to expanding the Australian economy. Simply slashing numbers will cripple the Australian capitalist economy, and it is very unlikely that capitalists are going to turn around and give "native" workers higher wages, better jobs and housing if the economy is going backwards.[20]

One of the difficulties in disproving the anti-immigration argument is that migration to Australia has been at a relatively high level for so long that it is hard to show hypothetically what would happen if it were cut. But there are some contemporary and historical examples we can look at.

During the Covid-19 pandemic, the borders were shut and migration to Australia collapsed to almost nothing. During this period, housing prices went through the most rapid increases in Australian history, thanks to the cuts by the Reserve Bank to interest rates. There are many governments around the world, both far-right and centrist, that are currently introducing savage cuts to migration. There are so far no signs that this is easing the housing crisis, let alone leading to rising living standards. Net overseas migration to Australia peaked in 2023. Since then it has fallen from 556,000 in 2023–24 to 306,000 in 2024–25 and is expected to drop further to 260,000 in 2026. Yet the housing crisis has continued.[21]

------

20   For more on the relationship between capitalism and migration in Australia see Humphreys 2019.

21   McDonald and Gamlen 2025.

We can also look at history. It was during the postwar period that Australia saw both a massive increase in access to housing and much larger levels of migration than today. On the flip side, in the wake of the Great Depression migration to Australia fell to almost zero until after the Second World War. As we have seen, this was the period when Australia entered into its greatest housing crisis ever.

The reality is that access to housing is much more impacted by wage levels, property prices and government intervention (or the lack thereof) into the housing market, than by immigration. The current housing crisis is a product of the contradictions of the neoliberal boom in Australia, which was fuelled by huge increases in wealth at the top of society while workers got by through increasing levels of debt. It is this which needs to be confronted.

A socialist solution to the housing crisis

The campaign by right-wing politicians, media outlets and think tanks to blame migrants for the housing crisis is a very deliberate one. They are seeking to reassemble a popular base for conservative politics that has fragmented in recent years and regain the political initiative from the Albanese Labor government. In the process, they hope to forge a coalition of radicalised racist ideologues, traditional conservative voters and discontented outer suburbanites.

The turn towards anti-migrant politics and the growth of the far right internationally is clearly a strong influence, with Pauline Hanson's One Nation taking the lead in trying to build a Trumpian politics Down Under. Labor has time and again either adapted to or outright capitulated to this campaign. To the extent they do stand up to it, they do so by pontificating on the pro-capitalist benefits of immigration rather than via a principled anti-racist and pro-working-class argument.

The socialist left can't defeat this campaign by accommodating to anti-migrant arguments. That will only disarm the left and strengthen the hold of racism and conservatism. In order to defeat popular anti-migrant attitudes, we need a bold, radical and insurgent socialist plan for housing that meets the seriousness of the crisis.

An important starting point has been provided by the Socialist Party. We do need to massively expand public housing and reject the bullshit of so-called "social housing"; rent caps would also provide some immediate relief to renters. However, as the history in this article shows, having more public housing isn't enough if it leaves the rest of the housing market untouched. There needs to be serious state intervention into the housing market more generally, well beyond temporary rent caps.

Much left-wing criticism of the housing crisis focuses on landlords and real estate agents. These are indeed the immediate figures that renters come up against. However, simplifying the situation as a struggle between renters and landlords misses the bigger picture. Behind the unequal structures of the housing market lie the banks, wealthy investors, development companies, the minority of landlords with large numbers of properties, all backed by government bureaucracies and powerful political parties, i.e. the Australian capitalist class and their supporters. It is these forces, and the capitalist system that they are enmeshed in, that need to be challenged if we are going to win some serious protections for ordinary people, whether they are renters, mortgage holders or home owners, from the vicious vicissitudes of the capitalist market.

In the past, access to housing has often increased because working-class living standards more generally have risen. This has usually taken place because the workers' movement and the socialist left have led and organised struggles that have pushed back against the bosses and won gains. As well, it is not enough to have access to any old home; we have to fight for decent housing that is worth living in. This goes back to the very construction of housing and its maintenance. Also it is little use getting access to housing if that means being crushed by rising debts, turning a home into a trap. So the struggle over housing will not be narrowly about this issue alone, but will be a part of a broader fight back against all the ways twenty-first century Australian capitalism screws over workers.

Throughout Australian history, there have been tantalising glimpses into what a struggle around housing could look like: the experimental Green Bans and housing actions by the radical Builders

Labours' Federation, and the floated plans of the BWIU for a nationalised construction industry, for instance. Ultimately, the real battle over housing isn't about migration or capital investment, it isn't about renters vs home "owners", it isn't even about Boomers vs Millennials and Gen Z. It is a battle for workers to democratically control the construction and ownership of housing. The solution to the housing crisis has to be found by looking at housing within the broader context of Australian capitalist society.

In order to really solve the housing crisis then, we need to transition to a socialist society. The wealth concentrated in the banks and the top property owners needs to be placed under the democratic control of the working class, and the structures of property ownership that straitjacket housing need to be abolished entirely.

This is an ambitious approach to solving the housing crisis, to say the least, but there are forces in Australian society that could fight for it if they were organised to do so. The majority of the population either rent or have a mortgage, and even most of those who own their own home are hardly in the top elite of society. There is a real basis on which a fighting plan that unites working-class renters, mortgage holders and home owners together against the corporate elite could be built.

The neoliberal boom in Australia, which began in the 1990s, for decades encouraged a retreat from class identification and a focus on consumerism and individualism. This has been eroded as the unequal consequences of this boom have become starkly obvious. Discussions about income inequality, class and corporate wealth have made a comeback. But the retreat from class politics during the neoliberal era has left its mark. The fragmenting of traditional political loyalties leads to volatility over popular understanding of the causes and meaning of today's inequalities. This opens up the space for the racist far right, whose arguments can draw upon long established conservative attitudes, but also potentially opens up space for the socialist left.

A new working class has been created, concentrated in the outer suburbs of the capital cities, working in hospitals, supermarkets, schools, transport, childcare and other industries. Recent migrants make up a large section of this working class, more so in Australia than even in other advanced capitalist countries. This is another reason that anti-migrant politics needs to be rejected, otherwise there is little hope of building a strong, united movement of the working class that draws in white Australian workers, citizens from migrant backgrounds and recent migrants.

It is important, then, to reject the arguments of moderate progressives who argue the left needs to accept cuts to immigration in order to win working-class support. It is also vital to reject the arguments of sections of the left who want to counterpose the interests of Indigenous people to migrants on the basis that migrants are "settlers" or "colonisers". No left-wing working-class movement can be built on the basis of either of these approaches.[22]

And while anti-migrant attitudes are unfortunately widespread, they are not totally dominant, nor are they unchallengeable. There is a body of people who see that migration is not the cause, or at least not the primary cause, of the housing crisis. A report by the Macquarie University Housing and Urban Research Centre in 2025 found that 18–34-year-olds thought that high interest rates and low wage growth contributed more to the housing crisis than immigration levels. Among this age group, rent caps, rent assistance and more public housing were all listed as more likely to help the housing crisis than cuts to immigration.[23] We should also remember that when Peter Dutton tried to win outer suburban working-class voters in the last federal election on a Trump-style basis, he was rejected.

"On the housing question, most socialists agree on the end goal: decommodified, publicly-owned, democratically-controlled housing for all – that is, dignity, safety, comfort", explain two socialist writers in a critical review of New York mayor Zohran Mamdani's housing policies. "However, there is significant disagreement on the means and actualization of those ends. What tactics, strategies, and organizations – what politics, in both theory and practice – are

---

22   Martin and Humphreys 2024, Humphreys 2022.
23   Wilson et al, 2025.

necessary to build the requisite power to reach our end goals?"[24] Taking on the housing crisis in Australia is also a political-strategic question. What kind of left-wing organisations do we need to mobilise the forces in society that can challenge the banks, governments and elites that are profiting from the housing crisis?

Our ability to tackle the question of housing and push back anti-migrant politics is dependent then on our capacity to start to build a mass radical socialist movement that can organise a fightback against the powers that be in this country.

References

Australian Bureau of Statistics (ABS) 1994, "Australian Social Trends, 1994". https://www.abs.gov.au/ausstats/abs@.nsf/ 2f762f95845417aeca25706c00834efa/f8f2b5b6a0447a77ca2570ec00787a54/

Australian Bureau of Statistics (ABS) 2021, "Housing Census: information on housing type and cost". https://www.abs.gov.au/statistics/people/housing/ housing-census/2021

Australian Bureau of Statistics (ABS) 2022, "Housing Occupancy and Costs: 2019–2020 financial year". https://www.abs.gov.au/statistics/people/housing/ housing-occupancy-and-costs/latest-release

Australian Bureau of Statistics (ABS) 2025, "Overseas Migration, 2024–25". https://www.abs.gov.au/statistics/people/population/overseas-migration/ latest-release

Australian Institute of Health and Wellbeing (AIHW) 2025, "Home ownership and housing tenure". https://www.aihw.gov.au/reports/australias-welfare/ home-ownership-and-housing-tenure

Buckley, Ken and Ted Wheelwright 1998, *False Paradise: Australian capitalism revisited: 1915–1955*, Oxford University Press.

Department for Communities and Local Government (UK) 2017, *50 years of the English Housing Survey*. https://assets.publishing.service.gov.uk/media/ 5a81fa8ced915d74e623521f/EHS_50th_Anniversary_Report.pdf

Forward, Carmen 2026, "NSW residential property: Regional towns where house prices rose most," *Sydney Morning Herald*, 29 January. https://www. smh.com.au/property/news/nsw-regional-towns-where-house-prices-soared-20-per-cent-in-a-year-20260119-p5nv8d.html

---

24   Rosenfield and Taylor 2026.

Grudnoff, Matt 2025, "Is population growth driving the housing crisis? Here's the reality", Australia Institute, 29 August. https://australiainstitute.org.au/post/is-population-growth-driving-the-housing-crisis-heres-the-reality/

Humphreys, Jordan 2019, "The political economy of immigration to Australia", Marxist Left Review, 17, Summer. https://marxistleftreview.org/articles/the-political-economy-of-immigration-to-australia/

Humphreys, Jordan 2022, "Review: Indigenous people vs. 'settler' migrants?", Marxist Left Review, 24, Winter. https://marxistleftreview.org/articles/review-indigenous-people-vs-settler-migrants/

Kuru, Scott 2024, "Australia's capital; city home prices on the rise of six quarters", Australian Property Update, 26 July. https://australianpropertyupdate.com.au/apu/australian-home-prices-continue-to-defy-tough-economic-times

Macintyre, Stuart 2020, *Concise History of Australia* (fifth edition), Cambridge University Press.

Martin, Oskar and Jordan Humphreys 2024, "Are migrants colonisers?", *Red Flag*, 9 October. https://redflag.org.au/article/are-migrants-colonisers/

McDonald, Peter and Alan Gamlen 2025, "Migration is falling fast – but election politics is spinning a different story", ANU policy briefing. https://policybrief.anu.edu.au/migration-is-falling-election-explainer/

Powell, Graeme and Macintyre, Stuart 2015, Land of opportunity: Australia's post-war reconstruction: research guide, National Archives of Australia.

Pullan, Nicola 2019, *Just a roof over their heads: temporary dwellings on Sydney's urban fringe 1945–1960*, PhD Thesis, UNSW. https://unsworks.unsw.edu.au/entities/publication/a94c4327-c64b-4380-98f8-a5b7b5cdf7ce

Rachwani, Mostafa and Antoun Issa 2023, "A quarter of Australia's property investments held by 1% of taxpayers, data reveals", *The Guardian*, 4 June. https://www.theguardian.com/australia-news/2023/jun/04/a-quarter-of-australias-property-investments-held-by-1-of-taxpayers-data-reveals

Rosenfield, Gen and Holden Taylor 2026, "Municipal Socialism's "YIMBY" Problem: the housing crisis and Zohran – which way forward?", *Spectre Journal*, 10 February https://spectrejournal.com/municipal-socialisms-yimby-problem/

Scanlon, Kathleen and Christine Whitehead 2011, "French Social Housing in an International Context", OECD Economics Department Working Papers No. 862. https://www.oecd.org/content/dam/oecd/en/publications/reports/2011/05/french-social-housing-in-an-international-context_g17a1fa9/5kgcd9s0q8f8-en.pdf

Sheridan, Tom 1989, *Division of Labour: Industrial relations in the Chifley Years 1945–1949*, Oxford University Press.

Troy, Patrick 2011, "The rise and fall of public housing in Australia", Talk from Proceedings State of Australian Cities, ANU. https://openresearch-repository. anu.edu.au/items/32928026-4295-4c57-9caf-2995e4da36cc

Wilson, Shaun, Ben Spies-Butcher, Adam Stebbing, Kristian Ruming and Alistair Sisson 2025, *Housing and the 2025 Australian Federal Election: Between Crisis and Inertia*, Macquarie University Housing and Urban Research Centre: Sydney, October. https://www.mq.edu.au/__data/assets/pdf_ file/0004/1357321/Housing-and-Election-Report.pdf

OMAR HASSAN

The Australian Socialist Party: A project to transform the left

Omar Hassan is an editor of *Marxist Left Review*. He is a long-term activist in anti-fascist and Palestine solidarity work and has written extensively on the Middle East.

IN JUNE OF this year a unanimous decision was made by the Victorian Socialists' conference to establish a nation-wide organisation known as the Socialist Party. The enthusiastic welcome that this new party has received has exceeded many expectations, with over 5,500 dues paying members after just 6 months, making it easily the largest socialist organisation in Australia for some decades.

We are well overdue for such a party. Economic inequality is at its highest point in 20 years as billionaires are still expanding their wealth at breakneck speeds and corporations enjoy unchecked power. All recent efforts to patch up the gaping holes in the social safety net all involve greater handouts to businesses – be they developers, energy companies, privatised care providers, and more. These subsidies and tax breaks have led to soaring profits for the bosses and worse outcomes for working class people, as demonstrated by the rolling crises in childcare and aged care facilities. Meanwhile real wages are falling or stagnating and standards of living are drastically falling. 99.3 percent of rentals are unaffordable to people on a minimum wage, while the cost of basic shelter keeps rising and rising. The right wing Labor government has overseen all of this, with the increasingly Trumpified Coalition parties – not to mention Hanson and the far right

– baying for even more attacks. If this wasn't bad enough, Albanese's decision to back Israel's genocide in Gaza and Trump's imperial aggression in Venezuela has made it clear that there are no red lines in the Australian ruling class' support for US empire and AUKUS.

This article will explore the context, rationale and basis for this new party, from the perspective of its largest constituent part, Socialist Alternative.

Growing space for a new left

The decision to launch a federal party arose partly in response to the promising electoral results achieved by VS in the most recent federal elections. Kath Larkin achieved the standout result in the progressive inner-north seat of Cooper, winning 9,000 votes at 8.4 percent of the total. Similarly, Sue Bolton, who ran on the Socialist Alliance ticket but was endorsed and campaigned-for heavily by VS, won a similarly impressive 8%. Both candidates more than doubled their previous results. In a similar seat in the West, VS achieved a solid 6.2 percent. This was only up slightly from the previous election due to a strong campaign by a relatively progressive and well-known Greens candidate. VS has always prided itself on seriously contesting in working class outer suburbs as well as more traditional left areas, a decision that was yet again vindicated when we doubled our previous result and received 6,227 first preference votes, at 6.4 percent, in the multicultural working class seat of Scullin. Indeed, it was in this seat where VS won its strongest results at the booth level, with booths in Campbellfield and Epping returning 20 and 17 percent respectively.

The party has developed a unique style of campaigning, which seeks to bypass the traditional limits placed on left parties, namely the deliberate disinterest of the corporate media and political elite. Instead we seek to mobilise and activate our sizable member and volunteer base, through doorknocking drives, mobilisations at polling booths, community forums, and other such means. While over a thousand people participated in these activities in the four electorates we campaigned in, much of it relies on the activist core of the party, to which I will return later. VS was also boosted by running Jordan van den Lamb for the Senate, an activist who has made a name for himself by producing witty anti-capitalist videos, particularly about the housing crisis. But beyond these factors, VS campaigners in all three seats reported increasing numbers of voters explaining that they 'always vote socialist'. It is immensely uplifting to hear people in their mid-twenties saying, as many did, that 'they've voted socialist their whole life'. This reflects the cumulative impact of efforts over many years, both during election times but also as part of street and union campaigns. In particular, VS has been centrally involved in the Palestine movement, with many of our key candidates playing leading roles.

The other immediate trigger was the poor election result achieved by the Greens. While their overall vote held up, the party lost three of their four lower house seats, leading to a crisis in confidence. To understand this situation its important to look at the party's broad strategy for electoral success. Since its foundation the Greens have poured resources into wealthy inner-city and regional seats, ignoring working class voters in the middle and outer ring suburbs. This was premised on an electoral coalition that combined younger and more left-wing voters with the upwardly mobile progressive intelligentsia, including educated professionals, academics, managers, retirees, bohemian types, and other white collar workers. While the former are prepared to be more radical on both economic and social questions, the latter tend to be far more moderate and are mainly focused on social issues such as climate.

The Greens clearly shifted to the left under former leader Adam Bandt, and some of their more left-wing MPs consistently supported mobilisations against the Gaza genocide. This increased their support among younger and more left-wing voters, as well as working class migrant communities, as measured in an increase in their primary vote in a range of more working class areas. At the same time, it alienated parts of their more moderate base, who swung back to Labor as the 'sensible' middle ground between Dutton's Trumpism and the 'radical' and 'disruptive' Greens. This was partly achieved by a relentless media campaign against the party for its 'extremist' stance on Gaza and parliamentary negotiations. The party was also squeezed from the right by Teals and Independents, and bled votes to its left to VS. Although its solid statewide results meant its representation in the

Senate remained strong, the loss of three quarters of its lower house seats allowed the media to crow about the dangers of radicalism.

These contradictory dynamics have led to much soulsearching and debate among Greens figures, and the future direction of the party is unclear. For the moment the party has bent back towards a more moderate position under the leadership of Larissa Waters and recently voted with the government on a package of regressive environment laws with only the most token effort made to improve them. Rather than passively watch these contradictions play out, there is a space and a responsibility to try and win working class and left-wing organisers and voters to shift their allegiance from a bourgeois liberal party to a clear socialist one.

These conjunctural issues have allowed the Socialist Party to gain a hearing in wider parts of the left than might have been thought possible. But the real reason to go national is that the capitalist system has badly failed working class people across Australia, not simply Victoria. Millions of workers have broken with the ALP in response to a long-term evolution to the right on both economic and social issues, as evidenced by its primary vote being at historic lows. Living standards have stagnated and in some cases fallen, while anti-migrant scape-goating is on the rise. This is not a purely Australian phenomenon, but is a broader trend towards the collapse of the institutions that have governed western capitalism for nearly a century. Globally, there is an insurgent far right that is now backed by substantial sections of capital, and here we have a new reality of a relatively insurgent Hanson-Joyce-Reinhart alliance.

There is therefore both an urgent need and a clear political space for a nation-wide alternative to major parties. And unlike the ALP and the Greens, whose organisations are entirely electoralist and over-whelmingly made up of inner-city technocrats, the Socialist Party believes that this alternative needs to be built among and led by socialists and working class people, and a party that actively intervenes into class struggle in all its forms.

Evolution of a political experiment

Given the Socialist party has emerged from the success of the Victorian branch, it's worth briefly recapitulating our history. Far from being born fully formed, the Victorian Socialist project has been evolving constantly. It began as a tentative proposal from socialist councillor Steven Jolly, who hoped to unite the two biggest socialist organisations in Australia, Socialist Alternative and the Socialist Alliance, behind a push to elect Jolly to Victoria's upper house. While Socialist Alternative had formally been open to electoral interventions prior to this, in practice the majority of members had a fairly dismissive and ultra-left attitude. The proposal for a joint campaign led to much discussion and debate, but eventually the decision was made to throw the group's efforts behind the effort to bring socialist politics into the political mainstream.

As it turned out, despite winning decent results in the 2018 state election, the coalition behind VS lasted less than a year, with Jolly resigning rather than responding to a grievance accusation of sexist misconduct. In 2020 the Socialist Alliance also walked out, preferring to build their own brand.

Thus by June 2020, less than two years after its creation, the party was at a fundamental turning point. The founding premise for the organisation was that a socialist party could only win strong results and real credibility on the back of unity between the city's key socialist activists, including figures with some existing profile. We also argued that the project was only viable on the basis that it stood an immediate prospect of getting a parliamentarian elected, which was no longer immediately on the cards. It was not clear if the party could survive in the new scenario. But it was quickly decided that those who remained had both the responsibility and ability to keep pushing forward on this socialist experiment. Indeed, there would be some benefits to being free from the shackles of the initial party structure, which were heavily premised on factional negotiations between the three founding elements of the party. As well, despite failing to get a candidate elected in 2022, the party emerged stronger than ever, winning solid votes across a number of electorates and substantially building the active membership and supporter base of VS.

VS has therefore continued to slowly but steadily expand its reach, profile and membership. VS has built its presence in a range of left wing campaigns, most notably by initiating a protest of 15,000 in defence of abortion rights in 2022, heavily mobilised for various pickets around Melbourne, and campaigned in defence of public housing. The Palestine movement has recently become a focus, with members throwing themselves into local council groups, student strikes, pickets of weapons factories and the organising of the main city demonstrations. VS members were key to organising the only two political strikes for Palestine in Australia so far, as part of ASU for Palestine union grouping. We were also proud to run Reem Yunis, a long-term Palestinian socialist, in a federal by-election to try to bring Palestine into the otherwise mundane political conversation had between the major parties. All of this shows that a socialist party can intervene at both the electoral and extra-parliamentary levels to strengthen working class and left-wing politics, and has helped attract a range of serious figures to the organisation.

At the same time, the avenues for members to participate in the life of the party continue to grow and evolve. The organisation gradually evolved towards a structure that allowed for genuine membership participation and control. This was not some smooth process. Indeed, we in Socialist Alternative were initially quite sceptical of creating a 'parallel, non-revolutionary party' that would repeat the failed experience of broad left party experiments internationally, a point to which I'll return. But as growing numbers of serious independent socialists put their hands up to propose initiatives and activities, the contradiction between wanting such people to be involved yet limiting their opportunities to do so became clear. So Socialist Alternative has gradually changed our thinking on this issue, and proposed to the most recent conference to radically expand the structures for member participation on the already-established basis of one member one vote.

Local branches and districts have now been meeting regularly, and are now electing their own candidates and establishing various local structures and committees. The Socialist Workers' Caucus has been established as a focal point for socialist trade union organising. Local branches have thrown themselves into campaigns to prevent cuts to community services, against the far right, and will continue to do so as issues arise. All of this is most developed in Victoria, where the party is most developed and well organised, largely due to the size of Socialist Alternative. But the hope is that this broad model – adjusted for local conditions – can be expanded elsewhere over time.

A new take on old debates

When VS was first being established, there were many critics, both inside and outside Socialist Alternative, who pointed to the disastrous outcome of other broad left electoral formations, including parties like the Scottish Socialist Party, Communist Refoundation in Italy, Respect, and so on. No disagreements there. Even the NPA, which started off more positively, has ended up being a terrible setback, as the party collapsed in bitter acrimony, with long-term militants lost to the radical left.

Like these organisations, VS does not require one to be an explicit revolutionary Marxist in order to be a member. It is a party for people who want to overthrow capitalism and achieve socialism, but it does not specify the exact means of doing so nor the exact vision of socialism being ultimately fought for. Of course, these are far from secondary issues. To win a better world, we will need a mass socialist party that is crystal clear on the need to abolish the capitalist state and replace it with a radical, working-class democracy. And if we are to put an end to imperialist wars and adapt to climate change in a humane manner, we will need to do this at a global scale. So it would obviously be a problem if SA's involvement in VS led to a watering down of our revolutionary politics and program to the lowest common denominator. But for now, there are no signs of this happening.

This reflects that there are some important differences between VS and the many instances of new left or broad left parties created in the last few decades. When the Fourth International consciously adopted its broad party perspective, it was merely the organisational reflex of a broader ideological shift to the right. This saw the organisation begin to abandon Marxism and adapt to neoliberal identity and 'movement' politics following the collapse of Stalinism. Much of the rest of the left, while not as consciously liquidationist, was similarly shaken by these events. For socialists with illusions in Stalinism, the fall of the USSR compounded the isolation and weakness generated by decades of one-sided class war by the rich, otherwise known as neoliberalism.

For this part of the left, creating parties that were not revolutionary was an alternative to clear Marxist organisation. The tactic of uniting a broader swathe of the left in a single organisation – which can be appropriate at certain times – was raised almost to the level of principle. Those who insisted on the need to build revolutionary organisations and maintain clear Marxist politics were dismissed as sectarians. Most of these so-called 'broad left' parties collapsed fairly quickly, while those that survive have politically and organisationally degenerated beyond recognition. The 'successes' of Syriza and the Workers' Party of Brazil represent one possible form of this degeneration, the other, far more common, are exemplified by the disintegration and right-ward shift of the majority of the old Revolutionary Communist League in France and the Democratic Socialist Party/Socialist Alliance in Australia.

For Socialist Alternative, the process of launching VS has been quite different. As previously referenced, the initiative to create the party was not ours. Rather, we responded to a new and important proposal – socialist unity around a real and practical project – with enthusiasm. Far from seeking to give up on revolutionary politics, there was a lot of apprehension about running in bourgeois elections and the cumulative impact of working with forces to our right.

After many discussions and debates, and the experience of the first campaign itself, the organisation has emerged clearer and stronger. We discovered that electoral work was not fundamentally different from other political interventions into student and trade unions, single-issue campaigns, and so on. Each form of struggle and activity has its own rhythms and challenges, and requires a specific set of tactics and strategies. But the basic task remains the same: to assess the possibilities and then fight for a program that can maximise the radical potential of a given moment or campaign, while simultaneously doing our best to bring a periphery closer to a broader Marxist worldview.

Importantly, Socialist Alternative also proved capable of recruiting radical workers and students to revolutionary politics through the various VS campaigns. This is premised on an insistence that there will always be a need for a clear revolutionary organisation based on Marxist principles, regardless of the other coalitions and collaborations such an organisation may participate in. Thus far from electoral work being a path away from revolutionary politics, VS was actually becoming a possible entry point to it. In turn, the growing strength of revolutionary organisation increases the socialist left's capacity to intervene into and shape the politics of broader society, be it in trade unions, on university campuses, in social movements, or in parliamentary elections. As it stands, despite the growth of the Socialist Party nationally, the capacity of the state branches to carry out initiatives remains fairly closely correlated with the number of Socialist Alternative members present on the ground.

A fighting socialist program

VS has been able to win a hearing due to our ability to raise radical but concrete slogans and demands. These connect with people's anger at some aspect of capitalism and simultaneously point to a more general socialist perspective. For instance our call for a rent freeze directly answers the needs of millions of working-class renters facing the current housing crisis, while also pointing to the need to take housing, a basic need, out of the hands of the market. Our calls to dramatically expand public housing construction, as opposed to the Greens' more ambiguous calls that include 'social housing' (privately owned and managed), builds on this, further emphasising the need to decommodify essential services. The same can be said about our approach to revitalising public health and education, the nationalisation of key sectors of the economy, challenging the systematic oppression of women and other groups, and our anti-imperialist foreign policy.

In the context of socialist electoral campaigns historically, VS policies are far from the most maximal. This reflects our assessment that slogans raised should connect to the most radical edge of left-wing sentiment, rather than pretending we stand before a radicalised working-class of earlier generations. It is a conscious concession to the reality of a greatly weakened workers' movement and the dramatically lowered expectations produced by years of right-wing attacks and limited defensive struggles.

Yet there is no sense in which this concrete program of action is a reformist program that aims to prop up capitalism. VS does not raise slogans which encourage faith in reactionary institutions such as arbitration courts, the police, or the military. We do not advocate an independent foreign policy but to end the US alliance and sanction Israel. We do not call for 'fair' wage rises but for wages to grow faster than inflation. Our goal is not to push for tiny changes through coalition with Labor or the Greens, but to be a voice for working-class and anti-capitalist resistance both inside the parliament and on the streets. As well, we always insist that our solutions are radical, and refrain from hiding or underplaying their anti-capitalist spirit in any way. And nothing in our program precludes revolutionary politics.

At the same time, as the party grows and evolves, it is increasingly clear that our politics cannot be confined to the immediate slogans of the election campaigns. For one thing, the party will need to be flexible, responding to new developments, shifting political terrain and new issues. Israel's slaughter in Gaza is a case in point, requiring urgent new slogans to be raised and integrated with the more timeless earlier statements on the rights of Palestinians to full liberation. So too the rise of the new far right, which will require the party to think through how it responds and what it demands of the state.

Inevitably there will also be deeper discussion of strategy and politics that arise as part of the normal life of the organisation. While the organisation should not become a left debating club but remain focused on activities that build its roots among the class, it is important that there be room for serious political discussions at conferences, branch meetings, and so on. At the most recent conference, for instance, there was a useful debate about the nature of imperialism, which the vast majority agreed was a feature of capitalism, and not simply synonymous with western domination. On a related note, Socialist Alternative remains extremely hostile to the authoritarian capitalist regimes that cloak themselves in marxist language, most important being the USSR under Stalin. Support for such bureaucratic monstrosities discredits the left and pollutes our organisations with anti-working class theories and practices.

It's not hard to imagine other future debates; the so-called parliamentary road to socialism, the best strategy for challenging union bureaucracies, and so on. One of the most important of these – a question that led to disaster in so many left parties in Europe and Latin America – is the question of refusing to participate in bourgeois governments. Socialist Alternative has and will continue to put forward revolutionary answers to these questions, particularly the latter, and we will continue to try and convince others of these views. Other individuals, tendencies and organisations within VS also have this right. If the party is to succeed it will have to develop a culture of collaboration on the basis of open discussion and debate, where the majority views are respected. The rights of minorities are already enshrined in the constitution of the state based parties, which should be reflected nationally as well.

All members of VS will have to continue to think through how all this plays out over time, and approach such discussions in good spirit. It would be naive to pretend that this process will be all sunshine and rainbows. There will undoubtedly be serious debates. Every organisation and individual will rightly have their own red lines, but there is no reason that splits or expulsions should result from every disagreement. As well, the sort of party that emerges from this process is far from certain in advance. Our hope is that over time this process can result in a growing membership that increasingly understands the tasks and challenges of overthrowing capitalism by revolutionary class struggle. One that can challenge the right-wing union leaders, and replace the ALP and the Greens as the party of the Australian working class, youth and left. It may also fall apart in bitter acrimony. But that is true of any political organisation.

A party of active members

The construction of a new socialist party of over 5,000 people in a few months is an impressive feat. But it comes on the back of 7 years of painstaking work that was only possible because of the committed cadres and youth brought to the party by Socialist Alternative. This has given the party a network of educated and experienced activists who are prepared to invest enormous amounts of time and energy into the project. Indeed it's impossible to imagine the party existing in its current form without the steady growth and development of Socialist Alternative over the years. The most obvious reason is the capacity for endless door knocking, letter boxing and so on of our highly committed membership. But it goes beyond this, with the organisation providing key political leadership from a local to a national level, driving many branch and state-wide initiatives, and engaging in longer-term strategic thinking.

This core has then provided a scaffold around which the party has grown to incorporate people with a wide range of experiences, skills and knowledge. If VS is to evolve into something approaching a mass socialist party it will need many more people outside the ranks of Socialist Alternative to step up similarly. The only requirement is that comrades be sincere fighters for the party and for socialism, an important caveat given that the organisation can start to attract sectarians whose contributions are entirely destructive.

An example of this process at work was the establishment of the workers' caucus to coordinate the trade union work of VS members. This was initiated by comrades outside Socialist Alternative, and fairly quickly won broad support as it proved capable of attracting serious activists from a range of industries. Since then fractions have been established in a number of unions, including education, healthcare, public service, community sector and more. The teachers group, Socialists in Schools, has already had some success in becoming a small pole of attraction for radical teachers and school staff, while the healthcare workers have helped lead a partially successful, though still ongoing, campaign to defend public health clinics in inner Melbourne. By fighting to organise and recruit leftists and militants to the party, and by popularising socialist politics in the union movement more broadly, these efforts can lay the foundations for rebuilding a working class left worthy of the name. As these groups grow, it is possible that their activities can begin to demonstrate the kind of working class power we ultimately need to challenge the bosses and their system.

Looking forward

The global capitalist system is in a period of profound stress and strain. After decades where the rich ruled for themselves and aggressively redistributed wealth from the bottom of society to the top, there is now a fundamental disconnect between the rulers of our societies and those they rule over. The old order is facing a crisis of legitimacy and control. Institutions of both the centre left and centre right are breaking down as frustrated populations search for new parties and politics to give voice to their anger.

This is also true in Australia. Despite a big win for Labor as measured in two-party preferred percentages and parliamentary seats won, their primary vote remained near historic lows. The Liberals are being torn apart, their moderate wing now largely an external faction (the Teals) freeing up the party's rabid right-wing to shift closer towards Trumpism. Meanwhile, mass support for independent and non-major party candidates continues to grow.

In this moment of flux, the far right has a project around which to unite the most reactionary sections of society. With its bold fascistic message it is achieving terrifying success in a range of countries and contexts, from India and Hungary to France and the US. These parties do not simply reflect a section of mass consciousness, they are actively shaping it in their image. They have built complex political eco-systems to propagate their bigoted messages, skillfully using the full capacities of the internet, but also through decades of grassroots organising and institution building.

It's time for the left to do the same. But instead of scapegoating migrants, dole-bludgers, trans people and women for our problems, our message is that it is the rich who are to blame and that capitalism is the root cause of all of our problems. We will fight to re-centre working class people and their grievances in a world that couldn't care less, and to aim their fire at the rich and their political servants.

We know that we speak the truth, but we will not win simply because we are right. Rather, there is an urgent need to build a network of activists and organisers to fight for this worldview. Elections have been the first focus of the party, but ultimately we will need an organisation that can take the fight well beyond elections, which in reality decide very little about the fate of the class struggle. Ultimately, to seriously challenge capitalism, we need a revolutionary mass party rooted in radicals at schools, universities and workplaces across the country.

The transformation of VS into a nationwide party can hopefully be a step towards this kind of organisation. For now, our goal is to bring unashamedly radical politics into the mainstream, to give working class people a socialist voice in parliament, in our unions, and in every sphere of society. We in Socialist Alternative do not pretend to have a full scheme for how things will play out in the long run. Building the socialist movement is never easy, and we will be blocked and slandered at every turn by the establishment and its hired guns in the capitalist media. But there is clearly an audience for socialist ideas and a growing minority prepared to actively fight for them. It's time to roll up our sleeves and get to work.

ANDERSON BEAN

Venezuela in Trump's crosshairs: Interview with Anderson Bean

Anderson Bean is a North Carolina-based activist, a member of the Tempest Collective, editor and contributor to *Venezuela in Crisis: Socialist Perspectives* (Haymarket Books), and the author of *Communes and the Venezuelan State: The Struggle for Participatory Democracy in a Time of Crisis* (Lexington Books).

THE KIDNAPPING OF Venezuelan President Nicolás Maduro and his wife Cilia Flores shocked people around the world. While it built upon the long and horrifying history of US intervention in the Americas, it was a sign that the Trump administration is taking an even more aggressive imperialist posture towards the region.

While the socialist left across the globe has strongly denounced this disgraceful action, it has also sparked debate about the nature of the Venezuelan government. When Hugo Chávez was president most leftists, inside and outside of Venezuela, believed that it was a socialist government or at least moving in a socialist direction. Under Maduro the government became openly authoritarian and pro-business, leading to a deep erosion of popular support.

While there remain plenty of slavishly pro-Maduro leftist commenters, ready to denounce any criticism as aiding US imperialism, this shift has led to many socialists becoming more critical of the government. However this opens up a whole series of complicated questions about the course of recent Venezuelan history.

In this interview *Marxist Left Review* discusses these issues with Anderson Bean, who has written widely about Venezuela under both Chávez and Maduro. He provides an account of recent Venezuelan politics that cuts against both the lies of the US government and the uncritical approach of sections of the international socialist left.

"The left's task is not to choose between imperial tutelage and authoritarian neoliberalism", argues Bean, "[i]t is to defend sovereignty while fighting for an independent, democratic, working-class alternative: restoring labour rights, freeing political prisoners, rebuilding unions, ending secret privatisations, and breaking with imperial capital".

> **MLR:** *On 3 January, the US government launched a brazen attack in Venezuela, kidnapping President Nicolás Maduro and his wife Cilia Flores. While this action came after months of building tensions, and there is a long history of US imperialist intervention in the region, it is still quite shocking. Why did the Trump administration do this?*

Anderson Bean (AB): Before saying why the Trump administration did this, I want to briefly dispel some of the purported reasons for this attack. First, Trump and Rubio described the operation as a "police" action and part of a "counter-narcotics" campaign, yet drug trafficking routes and data do not support this claim. Cocaine largely enters the US through the Pacific, fentanyl through Mexico, and Venezuela is a transit country rather than a major producer. As in earlier imperial wars, "drugs" functioned as a floating signifier – much like "terrorism" or "weapons of mass destruction" – invoked to legitimise unlimited violence without evidence, judicial oversight, or accountability. Also, just a month prior Trump pardoned former Honduran president Juan Orlando Hernández who was convicted in the US on drug trafficking charges.

Second, this had nothing to do with democracy promotion or Maduro's authoritarianism. Trump made this clear when he failed to mention the word "democracy" even once in his post-invasion press conference. In the same press conference Trump openly declared that Washington would "run" Venezuela until a "safe transition" was complete. After the bombing Trump also threatened the democratically elected presidents of Colombia and Mexico, these elections are contested by no one. Moreover just a month before the invasion of Venezuela Trump entertained the crown prince of Saudi Arabia, who has never won an election.

Third, it is not the case that Trump invaded because Maduro refused to negotiate. Maduro, throughout 2025, sought rapprochement, releasing US prisoners, cooperating with Trump's deportation policy, and offered sweeping concessions: dominant US control over oil and mineral assets, reversal of exports away from China, and the sidelining of Russian, Iranian and Chinese firms.

For the reasons that Trump did attack Venezuela there are several: Venezuela is a territory with extraordinary conditions for initiating new cycles of capital accumulation; to gain access to the largest proven oil reserves in the world; shoring up dollar reserves by preventing countries in the region from increasingly shifting toward trade and reserves in other currencies; immigration panic politics where much of MAGA has built its political identity around the idea that immigrants are responsible for social problems in the US and only removing Maduro from power can put a stop to it; appealing to the Florida, Cuban American bases in the lead up to the 2026 midterm elections, diverting attention from the Epstein case.

But the most decisive reason for the attack is a systemic one, it is a response to the US's hegemonic decline and attempt to reassert hemispheric dominance. It is part of a broader imperial struggle over markets, raw materials, trade routes and spheres of influence amid an intensifying crisis of global capitalism. The goal is to deny non-hemispheric competitors' control over strategic assets in the hemisphere. It is an effort to reassert US hemispheric dominance under conditions of decline and to use Venezuela as a demonstration case for the region, especially to discipline states that hedge with China, Russia, or Iran. Venezuela – cheap labour, dismantled regulations, abundant resources, and a shattered social fabric – is treated as both a warning and an opportunity: a place to expel rival powers and reimpose, by force if necessary, imperial order.

> **MLR:** *What has the response in the US been to the Venezuela attack? How have the Democrats reacted? What about the US left?*

AB: In the US, the mainstream response split into celebration on the right and procedural pushback from most Democrats. Senate and House Democratic leaders focused on how Trump acted rather than what he did: demanding briefings, citing the War Powers Resolution, criticising the lack of congressional authorisation, and seeking to constrain further military action rather than issuing a full-throated condemnation of regime change or Trump's claim that the US would "run" Venezuela. This is hardly surprising, given that Democrats and Republicans alike have spent decades undermining Venezuela: Obama initiated the illegal sanctions regime, Biden largely continued Trump's murderous "maximum pressure", and Democrats supported regime-change efforts like recognising Juan Guaidó in 2019. Even figures associated with the party's "progressive wing" have echoed this framework at times – Bernie Sanders himself once referred to Hugo Chávez as a "dead communist dictator".

A small number of Democrats went further, calling the attack unconstitutional or illegal, but these were exceptions rather than the rule, and even sharper criticisms were generally funnelled into procedural oversight rather than an anti-imperialist or anti-war critique.

The response on the US left looked very different. Within hours, "Hands Off Venezuela" protests were called in dozens of cities across the country. Hundreds demonstrated in places like New York City and Washington, DC, and even in small towns turnout was striking – I live in a small town in North Carolina where hundreds of people showed up despite the call going out less than 24 hours in advance. These mobilisations were explicitly anti-war and anti-imperialist, rejecting US intervention outright. Of course to successfully reverse Trump's imperial encroachments in Venezuela there would need to be a far larger and more sustained anti-imperialist movement both here in the

US and in Venezuela. Rebuilding a militant anti-war movement is one of the most important tasks for the left today.

At the same time, the protests reflected an ongoing debate on the left: whether opposing US imperialism requires political support for Maduro. Many of us argue it does not – and that conflating anti-imperialist politics with defence of an authoritarian, anti-worker government ultimately weakens the struggle against empire.

> **MLR:** *Delcy Rodríguez has taken over as the president of Venezuela. Debates abound about her role and the role of other sections of the Venezuelan government in the capture of Maduro, and their relationship with the Trump administration. What do you think about these debates, and how has the Venezuelan government responded to the US's attack?*

AB: I think at this point we can only speculate, but the speed of the operation, the minimal resistance, the failure to release transparent casualty reports immediately, the choice to recognise Rodríguez rather than Machado, the apparent readiness of the remaining leadership to continue governing and major concessions offered to Trump all suggest that sectors of the ruling elite were willing to sacrifice Maduro to preserve the structure of power. This reading is further reinforced – though not proven – by the fact that the US Department of Justice, in its charging documents, shifted from accusing Maduro of belonging to the "Cartel de los Soles" and engaging in "narco-terrorism" toward narrower allegations centred on corruption and illicit business dealings, a reframing that could be interpreted as leaving room for sentence mitigation or a future negotiating arrangement, whether contemplated before or after the capture.

Rodriguez initially demanded Maduro's liberation and used nationalist language about defending Venezuela, but she soon shifted tone towards "collaboration" and "cooperation" with the United States and a return to "normal activities". The defence ministry's messaging has emphasised calm and returning to work, not mass mobilisation or popular defence. There has been an increased military/police presence in the streets – more consistent with internal control and stabilisation than with organising resistance from below. This absence of mass popular defence persisted despite the fact that some mobilisations did take place, largely promoted by the government or by aligned sectors, but these were limited in scope and tightly controlled rather than expressions of broad, autonomous popular resistance.

Rodríguez's language since the attack is also striking: after a US operation targeted civilian infrastructure, that killed civilians and abducted the head of state, she describes her conversations with Trump as "courteous", conducted in a "framework of mutual respect", and oriented toward a "bilateral work agenda for the benefit of our peoples". Trump has responded in kind, publicly praising Delcy and speaking glowingly about cooperation and Venezuela's "future", as if the relationship were between partners rather than aggressor and victim. Delcy has gone further, repeatedly invoking "cooperation", "shared development", and even meeting with CIA director John Ratcliffe to discuss joint operations – language and behaviour that actively normalise US tutelage. This rhetorical normalisation matters because it blurs the line between coercion and collaboration, reinforcing suspicions that sectors of the ruling elite prioritised stability and regime continuity over sovereignty. Whatever one calls it – collusion or compliance under duress – it is not the posture of an anti-imperialist government responding to an act of war.

The regime's priority seemed to be stability and continuation – not sovereignty or resistance. What remains is Madurismo without Maduro: an authoritarian apparatus administering US demands under duress – a neocolonial state in practice if not in name.

Most revealing is the rapid restructuring of oil under US supervision. Under the new scheme, Venezuelan crude is being sold through US-authorised intermediaries, with proceeds deposited in bank accounts administered by the United States and disbursed at US discretion for tightly specified uses – effectively giving Washington leverage over Venezuela's budgetary policy and access to its most important resource. In practice, that is semi-colonial subjugation, whatever language of "cooperation" is used to present it.

The combination of speed, silence, stabilisation-oriented messaging and immediate economic reordering under US control makes "Madurismo without Maduro" feel less like resistance than managed accommodation.

> **MLR:** *Many on the left believe that the Venezuelan government is a socialist and anti-imperialist government. It doesn't seem like many Venezuelans have rallied to defend it despite the US's disgraceful actions. What is the nature of Maduro's government?*

AB: Maduro's government was not a socialist government in the sense that matters most: workers do not democratically control the means of production, and Venezuela's economy remains overwhelmingly organised around production for private profit, with the private sector dominating major areas of economic life. Even at the height of the Chávez era – during the commodity boom that financed real gains in poverty reduction and social spending – there was no decisive transformation of property relations, no break with extractivism, and no sustained confrontation with domestic and transnational capital; the model remained dependent on oil rents and global markets.

When the commodity boom ended and oil prices fell, the underlying fragility of that model became brutally clear. The key political question became: who would pay for the crisis – capital or labour? Under Maduro, the answer has overwhelmingly been workers and the popular sectors. While maintaining socialist rhetoric, his government pursued an increasingly authoritarian, anti-worker neoliberal program: collapsing real wages (from region-leading levels to near-starvation), weakening labour rights and collective bargaining, expanding repression against unionists and left critics, and opening the economy through privatisation and secretive deals that bypass constitutional oversight. One specific directive was Memorandum 2792 which labour leader Orlando Chirino described as the most reactionary and anti-worker legal instrument anywhere in the world in the last thirty years.

A stark example of this rightward turn is the Arco Minero del Orinoco. In 2016, Maduro opened a vast territory for mineral exploitation and invited transnational corporations to bid for concessions under extremely favourable terms – what one scholar aptly called "colonialism by invitation". The project has been environmentally and socially devastating, displacing communities (including Indigenous populations), poisoning rivers, and deepening a predatory extractivism that abandons the sovereignty and ecological commitments that once animated the best parts of the Bolivarian process.

This is also why many Venezuelans have not rallied to defend the government, even in the face of disgraceful US aggression. Under Chávez, anti-imperial defence could align with a lived experience of social progress and mass participation from below. Under Maduro, years of immiseration, corruption and repression have demobilised and fractured those popular forces, hollowing out the very social base that could defend sovereignty from below. The tragedy is that US sanctions and intervention have massively worsened the crisis and inflicted real harm, but Maduro's response has not been to deepen popular power and confront capital – it has been to manage the crisis through concessions to capital, austerity for workers, and tighter political control.

So the nature of Maduro's government is best understood as a corrupt, increasingly authoritarian, capitalist state that uses socialist and anti-imperialist language while implementing policies that resemble a rightward, neoliberal turn. That doesn't make US aggression any less criminal – but it helps explain why "defending Venezuela" cannot mean uncritical defence of Maduro, and why solidarity has to be with Venezuelan working people organising against both imperialism and the government's own anti-worker project.

> **MLR:** *Many on the socialist left would acknowledge that things aren't great in Venezuela but argue that this is simply due to the harsh economic sanctions on the country by the US. What do you make of this argument?*

AB: It is undeniable that US sanctions have caused immense pain, hardship and death in Venezuela, and any serious analysis has to include a discussion on sanctions. The most damaging measures – especially those imposed in 2017 and 2019 – cut Venezuela off from US financial markets, blocked the restructuring or issuance of new debt, froze assets abroad, and sharply restricted oil exports. These sanctions crippled PDVSA,[1] slashed foreign-currency earnings, and made it vastly harder to import food, medicine, fuel additives and spare parts. They did not create Venezuela's humanitarian crisis, but they dramatically intensified it and made recovery extraordinarily difficult. One well-known estimate found that sanctions contributed to more than 40,000 excess deaths between 2017 and 2018 alone, a staggering human toll that should never be minimised.

But two things have to be said clearly. First, the crisis did not begin with sanctions. Venezuela was already in a deep crisis before the first financial sanctions of 2017 were imposed. The end of the global commodity boom exposed a rentier model that had never been transformed. Instead of using oil revenue to diversify the economy and invest in domestic industry, the state massively expanded imports during the boom years. Local production was priced out, neglected, and hollowed out, leading to severe deindustrialisation and dependence on imports. When oil prices fell, that model collapsed.

At the same time, exchange-control policies became a massive engine of corruption. An enormously overvalued currency allowed elites – state officials, military-linked actors, and private importers, both pro-government and opposition – to access dollars at preferential rates. In practice, this meant an extraordinary transfer of oil rent from the state to private actors: every time the government sold $10, it effectively gifted roughly $9.50. Much of this was outright fraud – goods were never imported, and billions simply vanished. Two of Chávez's former ministers, Jorge Giordani and Héctor Navarro, calculated that the government cannot account for over $300 billion – nearly a third of the roughly $1 trillion in revenue collected over a decade.

Then there is the question of foreign debt. While ordinary Venezuelans were earning starvation wages, prices were exploding, and three out of four people reported losing weight because they couldn't afford enough food; the government slashed imports of food,

---

1   Petróleos de Venezuela, S.A., the state-owned oil and gas company of Venezuela.

medicine, and public services. Yet at the same time, PDVSA paid roughly $2 billion to international bondholders. This wasn't about fear of default – Venezuela was already treated as being in default by most non-Wall Street creditors. Rather, the crisis itself became a site of accumulation, with insiders buying discounted bonds and benefiting personally from repayment. In 2017, the Washington Post even dubbed Venezuela "Wall Street's favourite socialist revolution" because of the regime's priority of debt repayment over social needs.

Second, even acknowledging the devastating impact of sanctions does not excuse or explain Maduro's authoritarian and anti-worker turn. Sanctions did not require banning left parties from elections, jailing union activists, or repressing independent media. They did not require dismantling collective bargaining, allowing employers to unilaterally change labour conditions and fire workers, or arresting hundreds of labour leaders who resisted these measures. They did not require creating special economic zones – endorsed by right-wing business federations – where labour, environmental and fiscal laws are suspended. They did not require the Anti-Blockade Law, which effect- ively bypasses constitutional oversight and enables secret deals with capital. And they certainly did not require reversing Chávez's nationalisations and returning to privatisation policies that resemble the Fourth Republic[2] far more than the Bolivarian project.

So the argument that "sanctions explain everything" ultimately obscures more than it clarifies. Sanctions have been criminal and devastating and opposing them is essential. But the crisis is the result of both imperial aggression and a domestic project that chose to make workers pay for the collapse while protecting capital, debt holders, and a corrupt bureaucratic elite. Treating sanctions as the sole cause ends up absolving policies that dismantled popular power, hollowed out the economy, and left Venezuela more vulnerable – not less – to imperial domination.

---

2   A coalition government that was in power from 1958 until 1999.

> **MLR:** *Some defenders of Maduro argue that raising criticisms of his government simply aids US imperialism. Why is it important to be honest about the nature of the Venezuelan government while also opposing the machinations of the US?*

AB: Because truth is not a luxury for the left – it's a condition for effective anti-imperialism. Defending Venezuela from US aggression does not require defending Nicolás Maduro's government, and conflating the two ultimately weakens both anti-war politics abroad and working-class struggles inside Venezuela. In the same way that defending Iraq and Afghanistan against US imperialism did not require giving political support to Saddam Hussein or the Taliban.

The left's task is not to choose between imperial tutelage and authoritarian neoliberalism. It is to defend sovereignty while fighting for an independent, democratic, working-class alternative: restoring labour rights, freeing political prisoners, rebuilding unions, ending secret privatisations, and breaking with imperial capital. Maduro's record matters here because his anti-worker, neoliberal turn did not protect Venezuela from imperialism – it made imperial domination easier. By hollowing out the Bolivarian process, repressing unions and the left, pulverising wages, and governing through opaque deals, the regime dismantled the very social forces capable of defending sovereignty from below.

This is why January 3 was possible. The US assault collided with a society exhausted by years of austerity, repression, and abandonment of popular emancipation. Under Chávez, an external attack would likely have triggered mass mobilisation. Under Maduro, anti-imperialist sentiment fractured. Many people were demoralised, atomised, or even tempted by the illusion that US intervention might offer an escape. That illusion is tragic – but it was produced by the government's own policies.

Honest criticism is also essential because imperialism is not just sanctions or bombs. It operates through finance, debt, capital flight, transnational corporations, and domestic elites whose interests are deeply intertwined with imperial capital. Workers fighting unjust dismissals by transnationals, environmentalists resisting extractivism, and those demanding transparency in oil contracts are not "helping imperialism" – they are part of the anti-imperialist struggle. What weakens that struggle is treating secret privatisations, debt repayment to foreign creditors, and repression of labour as somehow anti-imperialist simply because the government uses radical rhetoric.

Maduro's own conduct makes this clear. In recent years he offered sweeping concessions to US capital – dominant control over oil and minerals, preferential contracts and strategic realignment – proposals that were plainly neocolonial. That is not resistance; it is alignment offered from Caracas. Rhetorical denunciations of imperialism ring hollow when paired with policies that subordinate workers, protect foreign capital's assets, and hollow out popular power.

Finally, there is a political cost to dishonesty. Defending Maduro as "socialist" alienates Venezuelan workers and left militants who have lived through wage collapse, repression, and the destruction of collective bargaining. It also undermines international solidarity: we cannot build a credible anti-war movement if we ask people to suspend their judgment about an authoritarian, capitalist government.

As Amílcar Cabral[3] warned: "Hide nothing from the masses... Mask no difficulties, mistakes, failures". Telling the truth about Maduro does not aid US imperialism. It is a prerequisite for opposing it seriously.

> **MLR:** *Many socialists were inspired by Hugo Chávez and the Bolivarian Revolution of the early 2000s. Where did Chávez come from, and what was the Bolivarian Revolution?*

AB: Hugo Chávez emerged from the crisis of Venezuela's old political order. Born in rural poverty in Sabaneta, Barinas, he came of age amid the exhaustion of the two-party system (AD–COPEI), the imposition of neoliberal austerity, and the popular explosion of the Caracazo in 1989. His failed 1992 military uprising – aimed at that discredited order – turned him into a national figure, and his 1998 election channelled a

---

3   Amílcar Lopes Cabral (1924–1973) was a Bissau-Guinean and Cape Verdean political organiser, widely regarded as one of Africa's foremost anti-colonial leaders.

broad, bottom-up demand for social change, national sovereignty and deeper democracy. The Bolivarian Process that followed drew on a heterogeneous mix of influences – Simón Bolívar and Ezequiel Zamora, anti-imperial nationalism, currents of socialism from below, and popular Christianity – rooted above all in the lived experience of Venezuela's poor.

There was much to be inspired by in the early 2000s. Using oil revenues during a global commodity boom, Chávez's governments dramatically expanded social spending and improved living conditions. Poverty was cut sharply and extreme poverty fell even faster; inequality dropped to among the lowest in the region. Millions gained access to healthcare for the first time through the social missions; college enrolment doubled; pensions expanded; child malnutrition declined; unemployment fell; and Venezuela rose in regional human-development rankings. New institutions – communal councils, communes, experiments in workers' control, and popular assemblies – gave real substance to participatory democracy and mobilised millions. These advances explain why so many socialists joined the PSUV [United Socialist Party of Venezuela] and defended the process against coups, lockouts, and US intervention.

At the same time, the Bolivarian Revolution had structural limits that matter for understanding what came later. Much of Chávez's tenure coincided with extraordinarily high oil prices, which allowed major redistribution without having to confront the capitalist class in any serious way. There was no meaningful transformation of social property relations, no change in the international division of labour, and no sustained challenge to the prerogatives of transnational capital. Crucially, there was no break with extractivism – the reliance on exporting largely unprocessed hydrocarbons and minerals – and no reduction in dependence on oil. In fact, oil dependence increased, leaving the country more exposed to global markets. Roughly 70 percent of the economy remained in private hands, and production continued to be organised around profitability rather than democratic worker control.

Those contradictions don't negate the real gains or the genuine popular energy of the early Bolivarian years. They help explain both why the process inspired a generation – and why, once the commodity boom ended and leadership changed, its achievements proved fragile. The early revolution opened spaces for popular power and redistribution; it did not complete a transition away from rentier capitalism.

> **MLR:** *What stayed the same and what shifted under Maduro?*

AB: Under Maduro, two fundamental features of Venezuela's political economy remained the same: rentierism and dependence on oil. Like Chávez, Maduro governed a country whose economy was overwhelmingly structured around hydrocarbon exports and access to oil rents, with little success in diversifying production or breaking dependence on global commodity markets. The promise of "endogenous development" and moving beyond oil was never realised, and in fact Venezuela's dependence on hydrocarbons deepened over time.

What shifted sharply under Maduro was the direction of economic policy and the political regime built to enforce it. Chávez's final years already showed tensions and contradictions, but after his death in 2013 those forces pushing alternatives to neoliberalism weakened decisively. Maduro largely abandoned the anti-neoliberal orientation that had at least partially defined the Bolivarian project and instead oversaw a return to policies resembling those of the Fourth Republic: market liberalisation, privatisation, labour flexibilisation, and the subordination of social rights to capital accumulation – while maintaining radical and socialist rhetoric.

Economically, this shift was catastrophic. Venezuela experienced one of the worst peacetime collapses in modern history: GDP contracted by more than 50 percent in seven years, industrial capacity collapsed, and real wages fell by 96–99 percent. The minimum wage dropped to just a few dollars a month while the cost of basic food baskets soared into the hundreds. This wage collapse drove the mass migration of over seven million people. While US sanctions from 2017 onward dramatically worsened the crisis, the core features of the collapse were already rooted in policy choices, mismanagement, corruption, and the failure of productive transformation.

One of the clearest ruptures was the turn to neoliberal extractivism, exemplified by the Arco Minero del Orinoco. Maduro opened vast swathes of national territory – over 12 percent of the country – to multinational mining interests under conditions that violated constitutional protections, Indigenous rights, labour law, and environmental safeguards. This represented not continuity with Chávez's resource nationalism but a reversal toward denationalisation and external control, subordinating disputes to international tribunals and creating extractive enclaves akin to neoliberal free zones.

Labour policy also marked a decisive break. Memorandum 2792 effectively wiped out collective bargaining, flattened wage scales, and dismantled decades of worker gains. Repression of unions, suspension of union elections, and criminalisation of dissent accompanied this economic turn.

Politically, Maduro consolidated an authoritarian regime. Laws like the Anti-Blockade Law suspended constitutional oversight, enabled secret contracts and privatisations, and concentrated extraordinary powers in the executive. Democratic checks weakened, transparency vanished, and repression became routine.

In short, what stayed the same was Venezuela's rentier foundation and oil dependence. What changed was the abandonment of even partial attempts to transcend neoliberalism, replaced by an authoritarian model that redistributed income upward, dismantled labour rights, deepened extractivism, and governed through repression – producing economic collapse while hollowing out the original emancipatory promise of the Bolivarian Revolution.

> **MLR:** *The early 2000s in Venezuela also opened up important opportunities for mass struggle and for the revolutionary left. Your forthcoming book collects a number of articles and debates among the Venezuelan revolutionary left about this period and afterwards. What were some of the revolutionary organisations in Venezuela at this time? What are some of the issues they were discussing and debating? What challenges did they face? How did the revolutionary left respond to the rise of Chávez?*

AB: In Venezuela's early 2000s, "revolutionary organisations" can mean different things, but if we take it to refer to left organisations that accompanied (and often contested within) the Chavista process, there were several key forces. Chavismo itself had shifting organisational forms: first the MBR-200, then the Fifth Republic Movement (MVR), and later other Chavista vehicles. Around Chávez there was also the broader bloc he called the Great Patriotic Pole, which included parties like Patria Para Todos (PPT), the Communist Party of Venezuela (PCV), and, early on, the Movement for Socialism (MAS), which participated initially and then broke around 2002. Beyond those, there were important revolutionary and radical currents that developed in relation to the process: Trotskyist traditions that had passed through the PST and La Chispa later regrouped into formations such as the Party for Socialism and Liberation (PSL) and other currents that eventually helped form spaces like Marea Socialista (including a period of work inside the PSUV for some). Newer radical Chavista formations also emerged later, such as Redes (linked to Juan Barreto) and currents like Proyecto Nuestra América/Movimiento 13 de Abril associated with Carlos Lanz, alongside figures like Roland Denis. There were also smaller but socially rooted movements such as the Ezequiel Zamora Peasant Front, community-based formations (e.g. Communities in Command), alternative/community media networks, and localised militant groups like Lina Ron's current and the Tupamaros, which often acted as satellites of Chavismo. Outside Chávez's own party, the most significant organised forces in that period were generally the PPT and the PCV.

The debates were shaped by the rapidly changing character of Chávez's project. After Chávez's 1998 victory and 1999 inauguration, a central early debate was nationalism versus socialism. In the initial phase, Chávez largely framed his project as Bolivarian, democratic, and anti-neoliberal – criticising the Fourth Republic and pushing a constituent process – but not yet explicitly socialist or anti-capitalist. He even used language close to a "third way" logic: as much market as possible and as much state as necessary. The revolutionary left argued over how to relate to this: was it a progressive nationalist movement to support critically, or did it require an independent socialist strategy from the start?

After the 2002 coup attempt, the struggle over the process sharpened. With the Constitution and major reforms like the Hydrocarbons Law and the Land Law, and especially from 2004 onward, Chávez increasingly adopted anti-imperialist language, began speaking of socialism, and deepened ties with Cuba. This shifted debates again: how to push the process beyond nationalism toward socialism, and what kind of socialism that would be. Another major axis of debate concerned the working class: its real protagonism, workers' control, union autonomy, and whether popular power (communes, councils, workplace organisation) would deepen or be subordinated to party-state structures. The revolutionary left's response ranged from working inside Chavista structures to build popular power, to building independent organisations that supported the process against the right while contesting bureaucratic limits and defending workers' self-organisation.

> **MLR:** *How did the revolutionary left respond to the shift to Maduro? What remains of the socialist left in Venezuela today?*

AB: Initially in the early years of Maduro, after Chávez's death, much of the revolutionary and socialist left continued to defend the Bolivarian process while pushing it to the left. But as Maduro's government deepened its authoritarian and neoliberal turn – wage collapse, dismantling of collective bargaining, privatisations, repression of unions and critics – large sections of the revolutionary left broke with Maduro. Some currents that once identified as critical Chavistas or left-wing PSUV supporters shifted into open opposition from the left, arguing that defending working people and sovereignty required confronting both US imperialism and Maduro's domestic program.

Today, what remains of the socialist left in Venezuela is real, but weaker, more fragmented, and operating under harsher conditions. It has been weakened by (1) sustained repression, (2) the demobilisation and exhaustion produced by years of crisis, and (3) mass migration – millions left the country, including many organisers, union militants, and cadre, making collective action harder.

Even so, important left formations and united front efforts persist. The Alternative Popular Revolucionaria (APR) emerged around the 2020 parliamentary elections as a coalition of socialist parties, unions, campesino organisations, and social movements seeking a non-capitalist way out of the crisis, and it included currents such as the PCV, MRT, PRT, and others. Related efforts have continued through broader fronts like the Encuentro Nacional en Defensa de los Derechos del Pueblo (which includes groups like Marea Socialista, the PSL, PPT-APR, MPA, Communist Revolution, CUTV, etc.[4]), which has coordinated campaigns among parties, unions and social movements in a united-front style.

---

4   MRT (Movimiento Revolucionario Tupamaro – Tupamaro Revolutionary Movement): While formerly part of the government coalition, a significant portion of this movement fractured and joined the opposition to the government (sometimes linked with APR forces) following "Supreme Court-led coups" against their leadership. PRT (Partido Revolucionario de los Trabajadores – Revolutionary Workers' Party): A minor, radical left-wing party that joined the Alternativa Popular Revolucionaria (APR) in 2020 to oppose the Maduro government's economic policies from the left. MPA (Movimiento Popular Alternativo – Popular Alternative Movement): Part of the coalition (often linked with the APR) seeking a new revolutionary alternative. It brings together grassroots activists, trade unionists, and social movements opposing the current government's, and the traditional opposition's, policies. CUTV (Central Unitaria de Trabajadores de Venezuela – Unitary Federation of Venezuelan Workers): A national trade union federation that has taken an independent, often oppositional stance against the government's labour policies, which have been accused of destroying wages and benefits. Aligned with PCV.

There are also newer coordinating bodies rooted in labour struggle. A key example is the Comité Nacional de Conflicto de Trabajadores en Lucha (CNC-TL), formed in March 2023 with delegates from unions and workers' movements across many states, aiming to unify dispersed workplace conflicts into a national push to restore labour, social and civil rights rolled back under Maduro.

One of the clearest markers of the left's condition is the state's systematic restriction of independent left politics. Parties such as Marea Socialista and the PSL have been denied or stripped of legal electoral status. Most dramatically, the state intervened in the Communist Party of Venezuela (PCV) – historically the country's oldest party and a Chávez ally – using the Supreme Court to hand legal control to Maduro-aligned figures, effectively banning the PCV's original leadership from electoral participation (now operating as PCV Dignidad without legal recognition). With that, the space for independent socialist electoral organisation has been nearly closed.

In short: much of the revolutionary left responded to Maduro's shift by breaking, regrouping, and building new coalitions, but it does so today under severe repression, organisational hardship, and the long shadow of migration – making it smaller, but still politically significant.

> **MLR:** *The Venezuelan experience seems to raise a lot of the broader issues of reform vs. revolution, and the debates around campism and Stalinism that has also been highlighted by the protests in Iran. What are some of the lessons we can draw from this history that are relevant to these issues?*

AB: A basic lesson – one the revolutionary left learned the hard way across the twentieth century in debates over Stalinism – is that you don't build emancipation by suspending criticism of an authoritarian state "because the enemy is worse". That logic tends to turn socialism into apologetics for whichever government is in conflict with Washington. But an anti-worker, repressive, neoliberal government does not become socialist by adopting anti-US rhetoric, flying a red flag, or aligning with Russia or China. On the contrary: when the left defends those regimes, we weaken our credibility with the workers and oppressed people who live under them, and we undermine the very principles that make anti-imperialism meaningful – democracy from below, working-class self-emancipation, and international solidarity with people, not states.

Venezuela also shows why "critical solidarity" can't be a slogan that excuses silence. Maduro's dismantling of collective bargaining, wage collapse, repression of unions and left critics, secret privatisations, and the hollowing out of popular institutions didn't protect Venezuela from US aggression – it made it easier. It fractured anti-imperialist sentiment, demoralised the social base that would normally mobilise against an external attack, and left many people vulnerable to the illusion that US intervention might offer relief. That is precisely the tragedy of campism: it treats dissent from below as a threat, when in reality it's the only durable foundation for defending sovereignty and resisting empire.

At the same time, the Chávez era also teaches a different, more complicated lesson about reform and revolution. The early Bolivarian process achieved real gains – poverty reduction, expanded healthcare and education, new spaces for communal participation – and it inspired millions because it opened avenues for mass struggle and popular organisation. But it also faced structural limits. The commodity boom created revenues that allowed redistribution and social programs without forcing a decisive confrontation with the capitalist class. There was no meaningful transformation of social property relations, no reorganisation of Venezuela's place in the international division of labour, and no break with extractivism or dependence on exporting hydrocarbons and minerals. Much of the economy remained in private hands, and the rentier structure persisted. Those limits didn't erase the advances, but they made them fragile – vulnerable to the end of the boom, to bureaucratic consolidation, and to counter-revolutionary pressure from above and abroad.

So the relevant lesson – whether we're talking about Venezuela, Iran, or any other flashpoint – is that the left must refuse false choices. We oppose imperialist intervention and sanctions without endorsing domestic repression. We defend sovereignty while insisting that socialism means workers' power, democratic rights, and class struggle from below. And we recognise that durable revolutionary change cannot be reduced to charismatic leadership or state redistribution alone: it requires transforming property relations, breaking dependence on extractivism, and building institutions of popular power that can outlast booms, withstand external attack, and resist bureaucratic degeneration.

CLARA DA COSTA-REIDEL

Review: Chile since Pinochet

Clara da Costa-Reidel is a socialist based in Sydney and has written on Latin American politics for *Red Flag*.

Robert Austin Henry, Viviana Canibilo Ramírez, Edgars Martínez Navarrete (eds.), *Chile 1973–2023: Contrarrevolución y Resistencia*, Volumes 1 and 2, Verso, 2024

MARX WROTE THAT capitalism comes into the world "dripping from head to foot, from every pore, with blood and dirt".[1] He could have been describing the birth of neoliberalism in Chile. Chile was made into a laboratory for reviving capitalist profits through violence – torture, murder and the disappearances of thousands of workers and socialists who dared to imagine a society organised for human need rather than private profit. This book assembles essays and memoirs by people who studied and took part in the struggle against the counter-revolutionary dictatorship and the neoliberal orthodoxy consolidated during the "transition to democracy". It challenges the official story of Chilean prosperity, bringing forward the experiences of workers and the oppressed in the neoliberal laboratory. For that, the editors deserve credit. We need more projects like this.

---

1   Marx 2013, p.533.

The project contains a range of contributions which cannot all be considered in this short review. Here, I focus on chapters that offer valuable insights and lessons for the left today, organised around three themes: the links between Chile's counter-revolution and global imperialism, especially Israel; Chile as a neoliberal laboratory that outlived the dictatorship; and the ongoing struggle against that order in the 2010s, and what the left can learn from it.

The counter-revolution's nefarious connection to Israel

It should surprise no-one that Augusto Pinochet's regime had close ties with Israel. Rodrigo Kamy Bolton details how, after the US Congress imposed an arms embargo in 1976, Israel became the regime's major supplier.[2] Even after Chile's return to democracy, local police continued receiving training from Israeli personnel; trade in weapons and surveillance tech also continued. Pablo Jofré Leal explains that Israel was chosen because it attached no political conditions to weapons trade, and because Pinochet personally admired the Israeli army.[3] Whether or not Washington wanted to be seen openly backing Pinochet's brutality, it could do so indirectly through its close ally. As German Chancellor Friedrich Merz recently summarised (in response to Israel's attacks on Iran):"[t]his is the dirty work Israel is doing for all of us".[4]

State repression in Chile is especially directed toward the indigenous Mapuche population fighting for land rights in the south. Mapuche activist and political prisoner, Matías Leviqueo Concha, describes the ongoing dispossession of indigenous land.[5] Land reforms won before and during the Popular Unity government in the early 1970s were reversed under the dictatorship. The "transition to democracy" only accelerated dispossession, with land taken over by private forestry and hydroelectricity corporations. When Mapuche communities resist these land grabs, they are met with police raids

---

2   Bolton 2024, in *Chile 1973–2023: Contrarrevolución y Resistencia,* Vol. 1, pp.105–16.

3   Leal 2024, in *Chile 1973–2023: Contrarrevolución y Resistencia,* Vol. 2, pp. 207–26.

4   Connor, Jones and Hairsine 2025.

5   Concha 2024, in *Chile 1973–2023: Contrarrevolución y Resistencia,* Vol. 2, pp.165–178.

and arrests. There is also an ongoing state of emergency in the region, heavily curtailing civil liberties in these communities. These policies are supported by right-wing and centre-left governments alike, with police equipment and training linked to Israel.

The neoliberal laboratory

The election of Salvador Allende and Popular Unity in 1970 was the result of a radicalisation, particularly among workers, throughout Chile. The new government was met with sabotage from the capitalist class and this launched a revolutionary process in Chile. Workers began building an alternative power at the point of production through the *Cordones Industriales*, which coordinated the distribution of food and other goods and ran workplaces under workers' control. They formed workers' armed defence committees and built networks to coordinate their strategy to fight the bosses. Chile's ruling class understood that to restabilise society in their favour, they had to smash working-class organisation and the population's hopes for a better world. That was the political logic behind Pinochet's violent coup – to make the idea of mass, democratic control over society unthinkable for generations to come.

They also wanted to reshape the economy. At the time, the global economy was entering into recession, and the capitalist class demanded a hard free-market program, based on aggressive privatisation. Garazi Zalbidea López and Estíbaliz Cuesta Burgueño show how dismantling social security during the Pinochet regime anchored the neoliberal restructuring.[6] Chile's private pension system slashed retirement incomes and entrenched inequality. Because "savings" are thrown into the stock market, pensions rise and fall with speculation. For instance, during the global financial crisis, a third of funds evaporated, devastating those near retirement. Women, who typically earn less and retire earlier, are hit hardest. Decades after the transition to democracy, the core of this system remains intact.

---

6   López and Burgueño, in *Chile 1973–2023: Contrarrevolución y Resistencia*, Vol. 1, pp.199–218.

Nicolás Ortiz and Rodrigo Torres analyse the neoliberal transformation of education.[7] Student federations were dissolved, university administrators replaced with military officers, and education was turned into a market. Higher education became a debt trap for poor students. The centre-left governments that followed did not dismantle this architecture but deepened it. They introduced co-financing that allowed public schools to charge tuition and enabled private banks to issue student loans with exorbitant interest rates.

Today Chile is the most unequal country in Latin America, with some estimating that the top 1 percent of the population own 50 percent of the wealth, while the bottom 50 percent own a negative share due to household debt.[8] This is the model the neoliberal laboratory produced and exported around the world.

The struggle against neoliberalism

Ordinary Chileans did not accept all this quietly. Students were among the first to regroup, rebuilding organisations under the late dictatorship and in the 1990s. Ortiz and Torres trace a movement arc from the 2006 "Penguin Revolution" of high school students demanding funding for public education, to the 2011 cycle for free university and an end to the marketisation of education.[9] The student movement politicised society, inspiring further struggle around the pension system and state violence against women.

While some concessions were made, the student movement was unable to change the neoliberal education system fundamentally. Ortiz and Torres suggest that this was partly due to the movement's integration into the political system. As many of its leaders, such as Gabriel Boric, entered into institutional politics, the focus of the movement shifted from the streets into the halls of Congress. Many student participants in the mass protests distrusted this turn, feeling they had more power in the streets.

---

7   Ortiz and Torres, in *Chile 1973–2023: Contrarrevolución y Resistencia*, Vol. 1, pp. 603–20.

8   Sanches 2024.

9   Ortiz and Torres, in *Chile 1973–2023: Contrarrevolución y Resistencia*, Vol. 1, pp.603–20.

Even so, student power and street protests have limits. Unlike workers, students cannot halt profit at the point of production. They can inspire and broaden people's horizons – which they did – but to confront neoliberalism decisively requires the mass industrial power of workers. For years, union leaderships, tied to centre-left parties, restrained that power. But as Chileans' economic situation worsened, pressure built beneath the surface until, in October 2019, it erupted.

A 30 peso metro fare hike was the spark. High school students occupied stations, jumped turnstiles, and opened the gates for everyone. Within days, hundreds of thousands had taken to the streets, paralysing major cities. Alondra Peirano Iglesias captures the mood during the protests:

We recognized ourselves in an embracing and overwhelming collective force in which profound yearnings for a just society and a dignified life germinated. We became massively involved in the uncertain and astonishing political process that was unfolding. We knew and felt we had awakened. (p.610)[10]

This was the most fundamental challenge to Chilean neoliberalism since the dictatorship. But, despite the explosiveness of the revolt, and some set-piece general strikes, it did not deepen into a coordinated strike movement capable of toppling Sebastián Piñera's government, let alone neoliberal capitalism. In the impasse, a secret deal was hatched behind closed doors between the parties of the left and right (including Boric and his Broad Front party). This agreement would channel the uprising into an institutional process to rewrite the constitution in exchange for demobilising the streets.

Ximena de la Barra describes the agreement as a betrayal of the movement that set in motion a years-long process that left the neoliberal core intact and even hardened.[11] At the time people were not fooled, and there were huge protests in the streets against the deal initially. But the movement lacked an alternative leadership, rooted in workplaces and neighbourhoods, capable of turning mass anger into a plan for sustained strikes, occupations and self-organisation. Piñera's

---

10   Iglesias, in *Chile 1973–2023: Contrarrevolución y Resistencia*, Vol. 2, pp.605–20.

11   de la Barra, in *Chile 1973–2023: Contrarrevolución y Resistencia*, pp.367–88.

government remained in power and the struggle shifted once again from the streets into institutional processes designed to neutralise it. The constitutional process was a failure, leaving the old Pinochet era constitution intact, pushing the movement into retreat, and ultimately shifting politics to the right. This was glaringly demonstrated by Boric's presidential campaign in 2021 which emphasised fiscal responsibility in the face of attacks from the right, in an attempt to win over the centre and business class.[12]

The lesson is that the capitalist state is not a neutral tool we can seize and wield for our purposes. Just as 1973 showed, its function is to protect the interests of property and profit; it will not permit fundamental challenges to those interests from the inside. Reformists, whose vision of change is limited to winning and holding state power, inevitably end up compromising with the ruling class in practice.

De la Barra is sharply critical of the movement's co-optation, but stops short of drawing the strategic conclusion the record demands. The constitutional process was not just mishandled, as she suggests; it was the mechanism for defusing a revolt whose power lay outside the state. Society cannot be transformed through a better-written constitution. We should see our task as organising the force capable of challenging the state's power: the working class.

In both the 1970s and the recent round of struggle, the force that was lacking was revolutionary socialists who looked to the working class to take power at the point of production, and who were capable of leading at decisive moments. The moment in Chilean history that came closest to challenging the structures of capitalism was during the revolution under Allende's rule, but then, as now, the reformist forces had a much greater influence over politics and the working class and this held workers back from developing and exercising their power to the fullest. The Chilean ruling class and its pro-capitalist backers internationally recognised the threat of workers' power and used this lack of clarity in the working class to make their decisive attack, setting in motion a period of aggressive class war that workers are still suffering under today.

---

12   "Chile's president-elect Boric meets with outgoing leader Pinera" 2021.

Conclusion

Chile 1973–2023: Counter-revolution and Resistance is rich with history and lessons. It shows the capacity of the downtrodden and oppressed to rise up and challenge the capitalist system. The project offers myriad takeaways for the left in our fight against capitalism today. We owe it to the courage of the Mapuche, the student radicals, the participants who faced down state violence in the October 2019 revolt, and the revolutionaries of the 1970s to learn the lessons of their defeats so we can be better prepared for the next rounds of struggle and defeat this rotten system for good.

References

"Chile's president-elect Boric meets with outgoing leader Pinera", *Al Jazeera*, 20 December 2021. https://www.aljazeera.com/news/2021/12/20/chile-president-elect-boric-meets-with-outgoing-leader-pinera

Connor, Richard, Timothy Jones and Kate Hairsine 2025, "Germany's Merz says Israel doing 'dirty work for us' in Iran", *Deutsche Welle*, 17 June. https://www.dw.com/en/germanys-merz-says-israel-doing-dirty-work-for-us-in-iran/live-72939104

Marx, Karl 2013, *Capital*, Wordsworth Editions Limited.

Sanchez, Jose 2024, "Percentage distribution of wealth in Chile in 2022, by wealth percentile", *Statistica*, 24 July. https://www.statista.com/statistics/1294731/distribution-wealth-by-percentile-chile/

JANEY STONE

Review: How identity politics ruined an important history of Jewish anti-Zionism

Janey Stone is a long-term socialist who has written extensively on women's liberation, Zionism and antisemitism. She is the co-author (with Donny Gluckstein) of *The Radical Jewish Tradition. Revolutionaries, resistance fighters & firebrands*.

Benjamin Balthaser, *Citizens of the Whole World: Anti-Zionism and the cultures of the American Jewish left*. Verso, 2025.

I BECAME AWARE of this book some time before publication. Having had a major interest in the Jewish radical tradition for many years, I felt inspired and immediately began to research the subject.

In earlier publications,[1] Balthaser draws attention to the little known anti-Zionist political positions of the Communist Party of the USA (CPUSA) in the 1930s and 1940s, significant also because of their substantial Jewish membership: Balthaser notes that an estimated half of the party membership in the 1930s was Jewish. Taking the turnover of members into account, some hundred thousand Jews may have at one time been communists, perhaps 5–10 percent of the entire Jewish population. This was particularly important in New York and other cities where Jews were concentrated, and where they were overwhelmingly working-class.

The CP centred its critique around Zionists' alignment with British imperialism. Leader Earl Browder argued that despite the fig leaf of a

---

1   Lazare 2020, Balthaser 2020.

mandate, "Britain owns Palestine and uses it to serve its own imperialist interests". Nor could Palestine provide a refuge for Jews, as Zionists tried to argue: "Taking Jews out of the hell of Hitler's Germany or pogroms in Poland and bringing them to Palestine...is not the way to solve the problems of the Jews".[2]

It was disappointing to find that, having drawn attention to the CPUSA's impressive political stand, Balthaser's articles provide virtually no insight into how it informed the practice of the party. This is a regrettable omission given that just a short search reveals some very interesting material about the actions the CPUSA carried out against the Zionists.[3]

A few days after 1929 riots in Jerusalem between Palestinians and Zionists, 2,000 Jewish anti-Zionist members of the CP rallied in New York in support of the Palestinians. A major campaign in streets and party publications followed, during which right-wing Zionists, Jewish socialists, the American Legion, and police attacked party meetings, and offices in New York and other cities.

These conflicts were often quite violent. For instance after the communist defence guard repelled an attack on 3,000 people at a rally in Brooklyn, the attackers called in the police.

> The police charged, brutally hitting left and right. More than a score of workers were severely beaten, one having his head cut open and another left lying unconscious... Six workers were arrested including Harold Williams, Negro District Organizer of the Communist Party.[4]

Despite this major shortcoming, there are certainly strengths in the book.

It ambitiously covers four discrete political periods: the Depression to the Cold War (1930s, '40s and '50s), the New Left in the 1960s–70s, Jewish identity politics in the 1980s and the (re)emergence of Jewish

---

2   Browder 1936.

3   See "Zionism, Palestine, and the Left: Articles from 1903 to 1939", Revolution's Newsstand.

4   "Zionist Drive Against the Communist Party", *The Daily Worker*, September 1929.

anti-Zionism in the recent period. Balthaser uses source material from a range of organisations such as the CPUSA, the Socialist Workers Party (Fourth International), Students for a Democratic Society (SDS) and its descendants such as the Weather Underground, and a number of Jewish activist groups particularly from the 1980s.

Balthaser's aim is to show that the current conspicuous involvement of Jews in the pro-Palestinian movement is not new.

> There has always been an antizionist Jewish left; indeed it is the emergence of a Zionist consensus, post 1967, that has been the historical oddity... (T)here has (re-)emerged a distinctively Jewish left that has held a remarkably consistent critique of Zionism... Jews on the left have both a particular opportunity and duty to ally with Palestinians and Israelis who wish to dismantle this state project. (p4)

Covering such a span of history is useful in establishing the continuity of this tradition. The high proportion of Jews in left-wing movements, as evidenced in the CPUSA in the 1930s and '40s, continued into the post-WW2 period. Jews played an important role in the Black movements for civil rights in the 1950s and '60s – in fact there was more Jewish support for civil rights than for Zionism in the late 1950s. Jews such as Jerry Rubin were prominent in Students for a Democratic Society in the 1960s and in other organisations of the New Left.

I was particularly intrigued by the activities of the Jewish radical collectives in the 1970s and '80s. Two such were Chutzpah Collective in Chicago and Brooklyn Bridge Collective in New York, which consciously looked back to the heritage of Jewish socialism and activism for social justice internationally such as the Jewish Labor Bund.[5] Balthaser considers they were important predecessors of today's Jewish Voice for Peace.

In 1978 Chutzpah pulled together a coalition to oppose Nazi organising in Chicago's suburbs, with violent attacks on Martin Luther King and other Black activists and local residents. When the city

---

5   For more on this heritage I recommend Gluckstein and Stone 2024.

government tried to counter their activities, they changed focus and announced a provocative march through a Jewish neighbourhood. Ultimately the march was cancelled, but not before the coalition held a

> militant gathering…(with) the presence of "Holocaust survivors" with "iron pipes under their sweaters" as well as Jewish and non-Jewish anti-fascist groups carrying "canes" and "baseball bats" – while most of the mainstream Jewish groups stayed away". (p181)

Subsequently an even more important march led by a diverse coalition brought together Jews, Blacks and a wide range of socialists and activists (including the International Socialists). Balthaser quotes a member of Chutzpah who "was privileged to experience the first taste of a fighting unity" among "thousands of Jews, Blacks and leftists…ready to brave…flying bricks and bottles in common physical defense".[6]

This march, which passed through a primarily Black neighbourhood, was violently threatened by white racists and resulted in numerous arrests. This was one of the largest marches against fascism in Chicago's history and the Chutzpah writer felt he was witnessing the "Black-Jewish working class communist united front" he had always dreamed of.

In sum, over the decades that he covers, Balthaser writes that "there was perhaps far more continuity with the three generations of Jewish socialists than there was rupture" (p.221) – a sentiment I can agree with.

But unfortunately, this is not the book for those who want to know more about this tradition.

There are three main problems. Firstly the book is heavily academic. Secondly, although while it purports to engage with socialist and Marxist organisations and activists of all stripes, the analysis is grounded not in socialist or Marxist analyses but in whiteness theory. And thirdly, although Balthaser is a committed anti-

---

6   Abramson n.d., "Confronting the Nazis", quoted in Balthaser 2025.

Zionist and supporter of Palestine, and his avowed purpose of rediscovering a radical Jewish anti-Zionist past is to be applauded, there is unfortunately very little actual history in this book.

Firstly, why do academics need to use words such as *metonymic, liminal, Gestalt* and *autochthonous*? If the goal of this book is to engage activists with a topic that is extremely relevant to our times, this kind of academic obscurantism is a barrier. It also reflects Balthaser's own barriers to understanding. For instance, in discussing a poem by a Jewish socialist woman about being a temporary white-collar worker in the new gig economy in the 1970s, he concludes: "The poem's Jewishness is perhaps its contingent relationality". I would think the poet had more need of a trade union than academic incomprehensibility.

The academic pretentiousness is however less important than the core philosophical and analytical approach – whiteness theory. Identity politics is so widespread today that it's not surprising to find an academic anti-Zionist who embraces and attempts to use the concepts to analyse Jewish radical history.

Sarah Garnham defines identity politics this way:

> Identity politics is a set of ideas and practices that aim to build recognition of and expand representation for particular identity groups. It reflects the social, political and career aspirations of a particular layer within these groups, who seek to hegemonise their political approach to oppression among all those concerned with challenging it. The starting point is the elevation of select identity groups to moral and political pre-eminence, while implicitly or explicitly subordinating others. Different advocates of identity politics see the world through different identity lenses, usually the ones that they are personally connected to.[7]

Garnham notes some general theoretical and political assumptions that underpin identity politics, of which the ones most relevant to Jewish identity are an essentialist view of identity and the assumption

---

7   Garnham 2021, p.83.

that the subjective experience of marginalisation is the defining feature of oppression. The concept of privilege is also important to Balthaser's analysis, rooted as it is in the originally New Left concept of "white skin privilege".

But Balthaser has a major problem in analysing Jewish oppression and antisemitism in terms of whiteness theory – most people would consider US Jews (most of them originating in Eastern Europe) as white, and therefore they would appear to be the bearers of privilege according to the logic of identity politics. What then do we make of the fact that Jews in the US have been the victims of anti-Jewish hatred and exclusion, not to say anything of the centuries of oppression they suffered in Europe?

The reality is that the position and status of the Jewish community has changed considerably over the past century.

In the nineteenth and first part of the twentieth century, Jews in the US were overwhelmingly working-class. As refugees from pogroms and persecution in Eastern Europe they brought with them their language (Yiddish) and their culture, including the tradition of struggle. In the pre-WW2 period and more so after WW2, sections of the Jewish community moved into the middle class. Although the tradition of socialism, activism and social justice remained strong, more right-wing tendencies also grew Zionism.

Marxists can discuss and understand how these changes in class position led to shifts in the relationship between oppression and exploitation within capitalism. But while Balthaser does mention class, his main analytical method is to try to explain social changes in terms of whiteness theory: sometimes Jews are "white", sometimes non-"white" and sometimes somewhere in between.

For example in analysing the politics of Jewish activist groups in the 1980s, he comments that their notion of identity is:

> relational, dialectic, and based on contingent relationships with both the left and other marginalised groups. The diaspora, then for (the groups) is a place between and among all these contradictions, neither resolving them nor allowing them to overwhelm the particularity of either group. Diasporism is

> neither exclusively identitarian nor a flattened, universal
> subject. (p 185)

How does this "sometimes it's one thing, sometimes it's the opposite" help us understand anything? The Chicago anti-fascist marches are successful and inspiring examples of how to organise, not a tortured academic subject.

Balthaser clearly had access to a wide range of resources. But the book almost exclusively discusses writings by individual members of selected organisations supplemented by interviews. There is almost no discussion of the politics of the organisations as a whole, nor are these politics really set against the period in which they exist. And most importantly, the politics are not discussed in terms of how successful they were – the analyses are abstract and philosophical. Balthaser gives equal weight to all the organisations he discusses, he maintains a distance (meant to make him "objective", no doubt), and makes no attempt to take a position.

The most blatant example of this is the failure in his discussion of the CPUSA in the 1930s and '40s to situate the organisation's politics on Jews within the changes in strategy that occurred in that period. The abrupt change in 1934 from what was known as "Third Period Stalinism" to the popular front strategy is completely absent – the word Stalinism does not appear in the book at all. This is a very clear example of the problems with the myopia of academic research: it often results in omitting core elements and context.

In the Third Period the Comintern, and the CPUSA with it, called the socialist parties and members of the Second International "social fascists". Thus the Zionists that they came in conflict with, many of whom were socialist Zionists like Hashomer Hatsair, were called "social fascist Zionists". This was in fact a major source of the violent conflicts. CP language changed dramatically with the introduction of the popular front, when the party oriented to building alliances with non-working-class forces and organisations. But there is no mention of this in the book.

In discussing the post-World War Two periods, Balthaser smoothly glides between discussions of the CP, SDS and the New Left, the

Weather Underground and the Trotskyist Socialist Workers Party (USA) without apparently noticing the fundamental differences between them politically. This is because the book is in the main a collection of material about thoughts and ideas in the heads of a number of selected individuals.

Perhaps the most famous quote from Karl Marx is from the *Theses on Feuerbach*: "Philosophers have only interpreted the world in various ways; the point is to change it".

Balthaser doesn't take us past the first point; the ideas in this book mostly remain in the heads of the people thinking them. But in order to change the world, ideas need to come out of people's heads and contend with each other – to be tested in the world. The value of history is to see how ideas are expressed through actions and group experience, to learn from the past. For that we need to look elsewhere.

References

Abramson, Rachel n.d., "Confronting the Nazis", *Chutzpah*, 15, p.8, quoted in Balthaser 2025.

Balthaser, Benjamin 2020, "When Anti-Zionism Was Jewish: Jewish Racial Subjectivity and the Anti-Imperialist Literary Left from the Great Depression to the Cold War", *American Quarterly*, Johns Hopkins University Press, Volume 72, Number 2, June 2020, pp.449–70, https://muse.jhu.edu/article/758945

Browder, Earl 1936, *Zionism: Address at the Hippodrome Meeting June 8*, 1936, Yidburo Publishers.

Garnham, Sarah 2021, "The failure of identity politics: A Marxist analysis", *Marxist Left Review*, 22, Winter. https://marxistleftreview.org/articles/the-failure-of-identity-politics-a-marxist-analysis/

Gluckstein, Donny and Janey Stone 2024, *The Radical Jewish Tradition. Revolutionaries, resistance fighters & firebrands*, Interventions.

Lazare, Sarah 2020, "The Forgotten History of the Jewish, Anti-Zionist Left: A conversation with scholar Benjamin Balthaser about Jewish, working-class anti-Zionism in the 1930s and '40s", *In These Times*, 13 July. https://inthesetimes.com/article/jewish-anti-zionism-israel-palestine-colonialism-annexation-apartheid.

"Zionism, Palestine, and the Left: Articles from 1903 to 1939", Revolution's Newsstand, https://revolutionsnewsstand.com/2025/02/25/zionism-palestine-and-the-left-articles-from-1903-to-1939/

"Zionist Drive Against the Communist Party' from *The Daily Worker*. September, 1929", Revolution's Newsstand, https://revolutionsnewsstand.com/2023/10/24/zionist-drive-against-the-communist-party-from-the-daily-worker-september-1929/

OWEN MARSDEN-READFORD

Review: When workers don't step up – a history of recent revolutions

Owen Marsden-Readford is a socialist activist based in Sydney.

John Rose, *Revolutions Thwarted: Poland, South Africa, Iran, Brazil and the Legacies of Communism*, edited by Alex Callinicos and George Paizis, Bookmarks Publications 2025.

"SELF-MANAGEMENT" – THE demand for genuine working-class control at the point of production – was one of the defining slogans of 1968. The struggle for workers' control inspired a generation of socialists and radical activists in the late 1960s. The late British Marxist John Rose was one such activist. In *Revolutions Thwarted,* Rose examines a series of revolutionary upheavals that took place in the late 1970s and '80s – the period in which the great hope of the 1960s and early '70s had been crushed by a reactionary tide and the emergence of neoliberalism. Rose sets out to test these struggles against what he refers to as his "1968 assumptions". Did they have the same revolutionary potential for workers' control of production?[1]

Across four case studies of mass struggles in Poland in the early 1980s, Iran in 1979, Brazil in the 1980s and 1990s and South Africa at

---

1   John Rose sadly died before the publication of the book, which was posthumously edited by Alex Callinicos and George Paizis.

the end of apartheid, Rose concludes that workers' control was not some relic of the sixties upturn, that "self-management resounded across four continents" (p.346). The energy and creativity of the working class in struggle shines through the book, especially in the numerous moving interviews with participants that breathe life into the accounts of the uprisings. They are reason enough to read the book. For instance, we hear from Kapuscinski, an activist in the Solidarność revolution of 1980, which he described as "an attempt to create new relations between people, in every location and at every level...the guiding theme...the principle of mutual respect (p.129).

As well as testimony like this, Rose's own revolutionary perspective cuts against the usual pessimism of accounts of revolutions in this period. Many left-wing critics of neoliberalism assumed it was virtually inevitable and wrote off the working class as a revolutionary force.[2]

Revolutions Thwarted is an important counter-argument. Even periods of working-class retreat, such as the neoliberal period, are punctuated by rebellions which open up the potential for revolutionary change. The global class war is never a totally one-sided battle. Notably, each of the four uprisings broke out after the wave of struggles from the early 1960s to mid-1970s had subsided. In each uprising the working class, from the dockyards of Gdansk to the mines of South Africa, moved on a scale that gave them the potential to lead social revolutions resulting in workers' power. Iran and Poland, where embryonic forms of workers' power emerged, represent the most developed of these processes.

This potential, however, was not fulfilled. The fall of South African apartheid, the end of the Brazilian dictatorship and the eventual collapse of Polish Stalinism, despite being driven by workers' revolt, took the form of negotiated exits to parliamentary democracy. In Iran, the revolution was hijacked, then defeated by conservative Islamist forces. These defeats were not just the work of outside forces. Many of the official leaders of each revolutionary struggle were not capable of or motivated to destroy capitalism. In different ways, their goal was to

---

2   See Harvey 2005.

restructure it. Some, like the leaders of Solidarność, even saw neoliberalism as preferable to socialism. In all four cases, the ruling class was reconstituted but workers remained exploited. New kinds of authoritarianism replaced the old.

This was not inevitable. So how were these revolutions thwarted? This is the question Rose seeks to answer: "how and why did independent workers' movements that played a decisive role in removing tyrannies in these countries…lose the political initiative?" (p.33).

Rose begins by charting the development of the theory of revolutionary politics and organisation from Marx and Engels to Lenin and the Bolsheviks. Two key concepts in this section frame the rest of the book – self-emancipation and the importance of the revolutionary party, and especially worker leaders within it.

Working-class self-emancipation lies at the heart of revolutionary Marxism, and revolutions under capitalism always point to this potential, especially when the working class plays a leading role. This is completely counter to Stalinist politics, which grossly distorts Marxism in theory and practice. Stalinists betrayed workers' revolutions across the world, from China in 1927 and Spain 1936 to the post-WWII uprisings. Throughout the 1970s and '80s, Stalinism was still one of the key barriers to revolutionary success. In the case of Poland, Stalinism was the active counter-revolutionary governmental force. In South Africa and Iran, Stalinist "Communist" organisations acted as forms of pro-capitalist reformism in the workers' movement, seeking to keep the working-class struggle within bourgeois-democratic bounds. In Brazil the negative example of Stalinism globally acted as an ideological barrier to the development and spread of an independent revolutionary politics.

Against this, Rose stresses the continuity of self-emancipation, from the politics of Marx and Engels to the revolutionary experiences discussed in the book. He writes: "[A] 'Communism' that claims to speak and act on behalf of the working class, without their active participation, cannot be the same communism that Marx, Engels and Lenin originally intended" (p.103). Great waves of struggle, however uneven, throw up the first shoots of workers' democracy from below.

The struggle for workers' control in all four uprisings confirms the Communist Manifesto's prediction that workers can "seize control and reorganise production in their own interests".[1]

But green shoots do not inevitably reach maturity. The workers' movements in Poland, South Africa, Iran and Brazil also highlight the inadequacies of syndicalism. To truly win "self-management", the working class must smash the capitalist state. Workers cannot seize the means of production without confronting the state. Rose charts how the syndicalist politics of the left of the workers' movement (particularly in Poland, South Africa and Iran) failed to rise to this challenge. Working-class power was never directed into a political challenge to the state which could pull behind it other oppressed sectors of society.

The missing ingredient was a Marxist party which could have charted a strategy for revolution. In particular, Rose explores the role of worker leaders in such a party. He defines worker leaders as those who emerge in independent workers' struggles. It is not a description of a few talented individuals but of the "most articulate exponents of a fascinating trend in revolutionary periods, the opening up to knowledge, previously understood to be beyond the reach of the ordinary man or woman" (p.338). Such a layer of activists emerged in each rebellion explored. Yet, the lack of clear revolutionary organisations meant emerging worker leaders were not fused into a cadre and leadership of a party which could have led to victory.

The task of creating such parties remains. For activists dedicated to that project, Revolutions Thwarted is worth reading.

References:

Harvey, David 2005, *A Brief History of Neoliberalism*, Oxford University Press.

Marx, Karl and Friedrich Engels 1848, *The Communist Manifesto*. https://www.marxists.org/archive/marx/works/1848/communist-manifesto/

---

1   Marx and Engels 1848.

PRIYA DE

Review: Conspiracy Nation – inside Australia's far right

Priya De is a long-term socialist activist based in Brisbane.

Ariel Bogle and Cam Wilson, *Conspiracy Nation: Exposing the Dangerous World of Australian Conspiracy Theories*, Ultimo Press, 2025.

JOURNALISTS ARIEL BOGLE and Cam Wilson spent years conducting research for *Conspiracy Nation*. They interviewed participants of anti-lockdown rallies, travelled to alternative lifestyle communities on New South Wales' Northern Rivers, spoke with families torn apart because loved ones descended into QAnon mania, and even went undercover at a "wellness" retreat hosted by former *My Kitchen Rules* judge Peter Evans. The result is a disturbing portrait of Australia's modern far right.

Conspiratorial thinking is integral to far-right politics. The "great replacement" panic, for example, conceives of a plot orchestrated by the "elite", Muslims, Jews, the left, and pro-choice women to eliminate the white race. Anti-vaxxers view public health measures as mechanisms by which the government, in conjunction with Big Pharma, restrict individual rights or inject the population with microchips. Sovereign Citizens believe the legal system is illegitimate and does not apply to those aware of this truth.

The take-home message of *Conspiracy Nation* is that conspiratorial thinking comprises a general worldview for the far right. Believing in conspiracy is more than a preoccupation with a single issue. Different conspiracies cross-pollinate the far-right ecosystem, all rooted in what Bogle and Wilson describe as "an explanation of events that places at its heart a secret arrangement by a small but powerful group of people to take control, to violate our rights, and otherwise undermine the common good" (p.7).

This is an insight into one element of far-right ideology and its recent development, however Bogle and Wilson's focus on conspiracy, and how individuals can be consumed by irrational worldviews, does not give a full picture of the contemporary far right. Firstly, *Conspiracy Nation* does not account for the influence of international developments upon the Australian far right, in particular the inspiration given by Trump's second term in power. Nationalism, economic protectionism, authoritarianism, militarism and anti-immigration are all central to far-right politics today and none of these are rooted in conspiracist politics – though they can easily intersect with it. In this way, *Conspiracy Nation* is somewhat stuck in the Covid era and does not fully account for key aspects of far right ideology, nor its political agenda. This makes the book limiting in terms of understanding the far-right phenomenon in its global and historical context. Nonetheless, it provides an interesting account of how far-right circles in Australia operate today.

Bogle and Wilson do stress that the far-right conspiracism is a threat, regularly accompanied by the potential for violence. Anti-lockdown and anti-vaccine protests emerging during the pandemic expressed this potential, with threats of murder repeatedly directed towards then-Victorian Premier Daniel Andrews. Conspiracy thinking implicitly and explicitly calls for individuals to take protective action to safeguard their rights against perceived threats. Such a worldview also lays the basis for lone wolf violence, which *Conspiracy Nation* explores by looking at the Train family and the 2022 Wieambilla shootings.

While it may be tempting to dismiss conspiracy theories and their adherents as belonging to the lunatic fringe of society, these ideas are connected to and sometimes bolstered by the mainstream of politics and the media. The interplay between centre and fringe is particularly acute when it comes to racism. For several decades, both major parties in Australia have deliberately spread Islamophobia through persistent policies targeting refugees and Muslims in the name of national security; a perspective eagerly adopted by the mainstream media in their reporting on domestic and international affairs. This atmosphere, Bogle and Wilson contend, nurtured the politics of Australian-born fascist Brenton Tarrant, responsible for the 2019 Christchurch massacre.

Tarrant's white supremacist manifesto betrayed the influence of conspiracy theories – that he was fighting the "great replacement" – as well as a racism not dissimilar to the suspicion of Muslims cultivated by the political mainstream. As Bogle and Wilson argue, "the line between conspiracy theory – the idea that elites or Jews or some other group are secretly behind so-called floods of immigration – and Islamophobia, antisemitism or forms of nativism can feel blurred" (p.73).

The establishment right, in particular that embedded within the media, can also lend legitimacy to conspiracy theories. Bogle and Wilson trace the conspiratorial undertones of conservative attacks on the Safe Schools program, an anti-bullying initiative aimed at LGBTI inclusion, that was a major culture war of 2016. The far right combined several tropes in a paranoid frenzy: Safe Schools was a scheme of the Labor Party to enable Marxists to turn children gay or trans. (Bogle and Wilson note that children are a recurrent preoccupation of the far right, as an empty signifier of innocence perverted by any chosen enemy, whether Muslims, trans people, or vaccines). Despite multiple reviews by lawyers and academics commending Safe Schools as essentially moderate and certainly benign, the Federal Liberal and State Labor governments agreed to gut the program, thus providing an ideological victory for conspiracy theorists and conservatives such as those in the Australian Christian Lobby.

Bogle and Wilson share further examples of mainstream politicians and the far right mingling in environments of free-flowing conspiracism. Former Liberal, and later United Australia Party, federal

MP Craig Kelly is quoted as speaking at a 2022 anti-lockdown "Freedom Summit" in Sydney, a conference of some hundreds from various anti-vaccine and anti-lockdown outfits. After mocking the Acknowledgement of Country, Kelly spoke about "...everything from vaccines and the 5G mobile network to wireless AirPods and central banks...the horrors of communism and renewable energy" (p.104). The leap from right to far right is not so great.

Conspiracy Nation also explores the normalisation of conspiracy theories in the "wellness" universe, in its consumerist realm and the communities built around "alternative living". The wellness universe is the domain of scammers and hustlers selling health, lifestyle and beauty fixes based on disbelief in and hostility towards modern medicine, science and state-provided healthcare and education. Emblematic is anti-vaccine sentiment. Bogle and Wilson cite that in 2020, Byron Bay, Australia's most popular alternative living destination, had fully vaccinated only 63.6 percent of two-year-old children, compared to 91.4 percent in the rest of New South Wales (p.130).

Diet and exercise are a common entry point for individuals into the wellness universe and a large consumer culture has been built capitalising on "natural" alternatives to those that are mass produced. But these grifters and their corporate backers regularly promote conceptions of naturalness, health and well-being that are fraudulent, dangerous and sometimes deadly. This world is based on conspiracist politics and has increasingly blended with more "traditional" far-right conspiracies. At the same time, its supposedly apolitical "healthy living" agenda has meant it has seeped into the mainstream.

Bogle and Wilson use former celebrity chef Pete Evans as a case study for the intersection of mainstream media, far-right politics and the wellness universe. He was retained as a judge on *My Kitchen Rules* even while promoting increasingly outlandish diets, such as "alkalised" water claimed to have filtered out fluoride. Evans was a major proponent of the "Paleo" diet, based on "the idea that modern life is making people sick and that returning to the habits of our ancient ancestors is the secret to regaining lost vitality" (p.189). Even after publishing a recipe for an alternative "baby formula" made of liver and bone broth that was condemned by then-President of the Public Health Association of Australia for being potentially deadly if fed to babies, Channel 7 allowed Evans to continue as one of the most familiar faces on Australian television. Evans was acceptable so long as his conspiracies were marketable, in the form of recipe books and branded ingredients. It was only when Evans shared a meme associated with Nazis on Facebook that he was quietly dumped from television.

Health and wellness, conspiracy, and far-right ideas dovetail around paranoia of contamination with the "unnatural". In the first instance, that might be unnaturalness associated with the body; in different iterations, the unnatural contaminant to be removed may be immigration impinging on racial purity, or left-wing ideas eroding traditional gender values. These ideas are transferable and interlinked.

Conspiracy Nation is an interesting product of good journalism. Bogle and Wilson break down the irrational ideologies embedded in the constituent elements of Australia's contemporary far right. The book's main argument is important: that far-right views, which may seem detached entirely from reality, are often sanitised or bolstered by mainstream politics and media. But because Bogle and Wilson limit their study to describing the conspiracist far right today, they cannot provide answers to the most important questions those disturbed by the far right have: where do these politics come from, and how can they be fought? Instead they offer by way of conclusion the valid but pessimistic observation: "After years of reporting, it's clear to us the narrative frames and the flow of these beliefs aren't new and aren't going anywhere, even as we can be disturbed by the pain that they can cause and condemn those who make money off them" (p.194).

Far-right politics are rooted in the inequality of capitalism, often presenting a radical version of the system's oppressive norms. These radical politics have gained currency internationally as the system has become increasingly unstable, with the state and ruling class in major centres of world capitalism grappling with sluggish economies, rising imperial tensions and social instability. But the instability and polarisation that can create space for the far right to grow also lays the basis for a renewed interest in socialist ideas and left-wing mass struggles – of which there have been many in 2025, from revolutions in Nepal to mass general strikes in Italy. This is our hope for defeating the far right: socialist, working-class struggle against capitalism, the system which breeds fascism and its attendant horrors.

When read with a Marxist framework to fill in the gaps, Bogle and Wilson's account of how the Australian far right thinks and acts is useful for left-wing people who want to fight these dangerous politics.

DANICA RACHEL

Review: The Crude Lifeblood of Capitalism

Danica Rachel is a socialist based in Perth who writes on local and international issues for *Red Flag*.

Adam Hanieh, *Crude Capitalism: Oil, Corporate Power, and the Making of the World Market*, Verso, 2024.

THE CLIMATE CRISIS is one of the biggest problems we face. The change in the world environment driven by the burning of fossil fuels and carbon emissions is devastating ecosystems and the lives of millions of people through floods, fires, droughts and increasing temperatures. The livelihoods of tens to hundreds of millions more will come under threat in the coming decades.

Confronting the centrality of fossil fuels to the world economy is of critical importance. Adam Hanieh's *Crude Capitalism: Oil, Corporate Power, and the Making of the World Market* is an essential resource for anyone seeking to understand and challenge fossil-fuelled capitalism— especially those wanting to grasp the central role of the world's most important fossil fuel: crude oil.

Structured as a history of late-nineteenth century capitalism to the present, told through the lens of oil, *Crude Capitalism* demonstrates that the dominance of fossil fuels is no accident, nor can they simply be unplugged from the economy. Crude oil is embedded in capitalist production. Its physical properties make it an ideal energy source for an economic system driven by accumulation and profit. It is also easily transformed into almost anything by way of synthetic materials such as plastic, which has led to its wide integration into commodity production.

Capitalism's perfect energy source

Capitalism is a system dependent on growth. The capitalists are in a life-or-death competition with each other to accumulate as much wealth as possible. They do this by investing their capital in a constant quest to make higher profit margins. Increasing the productive capacity, and therefore profitability, requires ever more advanced methods of production, as well as a higher throughput of the energy and materials practically required to produce whatever commodity. This core dynamic informs Hanieh's entire argument about the intractability of fossil fuels under capitalism.

Crude Capitalism's first chapter lays out how fossil fuels came to be central to capitalism. Coal played a major role in enabling the expansion and eventual domination of capitalism as an economic system. The invention of the coal-powered steam engine freed capitalists from the waterways and windmills they previously needed to power their factories and led to an exponential increase in labour productivity through automation. From the early 19th century coal-powered trains and boats expanded the market and ushered in a new phase of colonialism.

Then, in chapters 5 and 6 Hanieh explores how after World War II the domination of crude oil is consolidated. It plays an essential role in restoring profitability in the war-torn countries by facilitating cheaper and more easily distributed energy. The rapid economic growth of the post-war boom relied on oil as the fuel in its engine. Oil enabled mass electrification for households and industries, which opened up new markets of consumer goods and enabled more advanced automation in production. Liquid fuels derived from oil–used for the first time on a large scale in World War II–made coal-powered steam trains and ships obsolete. Improved logistics from oil-powered planes and ships brought the world market closer together, allowing multinational corporations to emerge and expand their quest for market domination around the globe.

The production and consumption of oil as an energy source has only increased in the decades since, and remains tied to capitalism's need to increase its overall productive capacity. From 2000 to 2019, global oil consumption increased by 30 percent, driven primarily by demand from China, which rose as the workshop of the world as firms moved factory production there to exploit low labour costs.

Oil's integration into the productive process

As important as oil is to energy production, it is not the only fossil fuel in wide use. Coal and natural gas are also important energy sources, and indeed renewable energy sources are coming into use in some sections of the world economy. But there is another dimension to crude oil's importance to capitalist production: it has become an important input *material*. Oil is the essential ingredient in making synthetic materials including plastics, synthetic fibres like polyester, and even fertilisers and pesticides that are now in widespread use in industrial agriculture.

The post-war period was not only fueled by oil, but was made of it too. Production in the advanced economies was reshaped around synthetic materials, which meant building large, integrated and automated oil processing facilities, with very low labour costs relative to their productive capacity. To increase production, the main thing bosses had to do was get more oil flowing through, not necessarily hire more workers.

Plastic in particular dramatically simplified the production of a wide range of commodities. Mass-production of plastic items only requires making moulds that can be repeatedly filled with plastic in highly automated production lines. Production was also separated further from natural processes. Organic materials like wood or cotton take time to be grown, harvested and shaped. Synthetics can be produced much more rapidly. For the bosses, this means faster and more efficient cycles of generating profit.

The use of synthetics has continued apace. Plastic production is accelerating: *half* of all plastic ever produced was made in the last 20 or so years. Synthetic materials have systematically displaced natural materials in households and industry. Polyester now counts for more of global fibre production than all other fibres combined. The carbon emissions from degrading plastic items dumped into the environment is staggering: plastic would rank fifth in total greenhouse gas emissions if counted as a country. Microplastics are accelerating global warming by decreasing the ability of the ocean to act as a carbon sink.

Crude Capitalism puts a spotlight on this under-emphasised aspect of oil in Chapter 7. Crude oil being a central ingredient of huge sectors of production means that even if fossil fuels were eliminated from energy production, oil would still be essential for keeping capitalism running.

Oil and imperialism

A constant through-line of *Crude Capitalism* is the role of oil within global imperialism. For much of the twentieth century (and to a lesser extent still today) western oil companies extracted great wealth from the global south, and in this way helped to secure the dominance of many western nations. The United States' domestic oil industry powered it to become the world's superpower for the second half of the century and it remains important for US industry and the military today.

The oil reserves of the Middle East are part of the reason the region has been the site of many conflicts between world powers, both hot and cold. The United States has continually sought to maintain its strength in the region by exchanging weapons for petrodollars with oil-producing countries such as Iran (until the revolution of 1979) and Saudi Arabia, and arming its brute-force watchdog Israel to the teeth. The immense financial surplus of Saudi Arabia from oil production even played a role in establishing the global hegemony of the US dollar as the world currency in the 1970s (Chapter 9).

The Russian Revolution of 1917 denied Western companies access to oil reserves in the Caucasus, a region second only to the US in oil production at the time. These reserves later powered the USSR's imperialist war machine through the Cold War and today fuel Putin's army as it seeks to dominate Ukraine.

Chapter 12 shows how the rise of China as an aspiring superpower rival to the US is also linked to oil. In recent years, the Gulf states have been establishing economic relationships with China, reflecting the declining dominance of the US over the Middle East, and the trade of oil and its derivatives is a major element. In 2018 China launched mechanisms by which oil can be traded on the Shanghai International Exchange in renminbi, China's currency, to attempt to undermine the dominance of the US dollar in the oil trade and financial markets more generally.

The ways in which oil weaves through the dynamics of world imperialism are too numerous to summarise here. The general point is that because oil is so important for profit-making, both in its own right as a commodity and in enabling production, control over and access to it is a concern of high priority to imperialist powers. And we can be sure that as the trend towards greater military buildup continues oil will continue to be central, as there is simply no other energy source suitable to power machines of war.

What solution?

Readers of *Crude Capitalism* will be left with no other conclusion than the one Hanieh reaches: capitalism must be replaced by socialism. The mainstream proposed solutions that operate within the framework of capitalism are at best inadequate and at worst a deliberate ruse. Only through the total reorganisation of every part of production on the basis of meeting human need instead of chasing profits will we be able to reduce carbon emissions to the levels necessary to preserve life and the planet as we know it.

Unfortunately *Crude Capitalism* stops short of discussing *how* capitalism can be replaced by socialism. Hanieh makes entirely supportable proposals that will doubtlessly be essential along whatever path is taken towards socialism: democratising control over energy; ending wasteful production; eliminating the world's largest source of carbon emissions–the US military–through demilitarisation. But these proposals are not brought together into a coherent strategy for challenging capitalist domination and the construction of a new form of society. Most crucially *Crude Capitalism* underplays the role of the global working class in achieving the social change necessary.

Workers are acknowledged as having a role to play in the transition from capitalism to socialism. For instance, some of the closing words of the book argue "[t]he central place of labour in capitalism gives a particular weight to the struggles of urban and rural workers, including those in the informal sector and outside official trade union structures." But this is misorienting with regards to which workers will be most crucial in confronting oil and indeed capitalism itself. That fossil fuels, and crude oil in particular, are so essential for capitalism's functioning puts the workers in the sector in a position to put the whole system in a chokehold. Oil is the lifeblood of the world's intricate networks of energy production, commodity production, finance, logistics and imperialism. Having it come under the control of the workers who keep it flowing would be one of the largest blows to capitalist rule imaginable.

As well as this Hanieh does not explicitly draw out why workers' unique social power gives them not only "particular weight" but makes them the *only* force capable of leading the struggles necessary to overthrow capitalism and build socialism. In the Communist Manifesto, Karl Marx and Friedrich Engels famously remarked that, in establishing capitalism, what the bosses create above all else are their own grave-diggers in the working class. If that is true, then the workers of the world's oil drills, rigs, pipelines, tankers, refineries and petrol stations must be among those with the biggest shovels.

Aside from these strategic shortcomings, *Crude Capitalism* is indispensable for its central argument that capitalism has to go if we are to avert the climate catastrophe. Understanding precisely how oil is woven through the fabric of capitalist society makes this absolutely clear.